Lake Of The Dead

STU DUVAL

Pearson Australia
(a division of Pearson Australia Group Pty Ltd)
707 Collins Street, Melbourne, Victoria 3008
PO Box 23360, Melbourne, Victoria 8012
www.pearson.com.au

© Pearson 2009
First published 2009
Reprinted 2009, 2012 (x3), 2015, 2021

Produced by Pearson
ISBN: 978-1-86970-650-0

Commissioning Editor: Lucy Armour
Editors: Elizabeth Hookings, Jan Chilwell
Page Layout and Design: Cheryl Rowe
Illustrations: Stu Duval
Printed in Australia by the SOS Print + Media Group

Pearson Australia Group Pty Ltd   ABN 40 004 245 943

STU DUVAL

LAKE OF THE DEAD

BELLEVUE FOREST WILDERNESS PARK

SCALE 1:50 000

WICKER LAKE SECTION SFS290   PUBLISHED BY DEPT. FOREST & SURVEY

Author Note

I have always been intrigued by tales of prehistoric creatures who inhabit the deep. The Loch Ness Monster, for instance, fascinated me as a boy. Still does. Maybe there are things that science can't explain – creatures that have survived a million years, lurking on the misty edges of our imaginations. I hope so, for it would be a tragedy if all mysteries were solved, all sightings disproved, all creatures discovered and catalogued. I love the idea that the Abominable Snowman, Big Foot and the Giant Sea Serpent of mariners' tales are lurking out there somewhere. The occasional sightings, captured on grainy film and snapped in blurred photographs, only make me happier. Why? Because they keep the legends alive and make us wonder, lying in our beds at night, if the tales our parents scared us with are actually true.

I think there is also a deep part of our psyche that fears such creatures. And maybe it's not that deep at all. I still freak out swimming across deep, dark water. Thanks to the film *Jaws*, I suspect. It is why we love to tell ghost stories around a fire in the middle of the night. The idea that "something's out there, and it's after me" is kind of exhilarating, in a weird way. So, long live the creatures of the deep, and of the dark, and of our scariest dreams and tales.

Lake of the Dead is my small addition to this tradition.

Stu Duval

Prologue

Excerpt from the Diary of Captain Ezra Bellevue
November 2nd, 1795

I have only hours left to live.

Yet, as I write this final account, I fully realise that the events I must record are so unbelievable as to be dismissed by whoever reads them as the ravings of a madman.

But I swear on all that is holy that what I write is true.

I am the only one of my travelling companions left alive and indeed my own life fades fast, due to my wounds and the gangrene that has now infected them.

1

Lake Of The Dead

Of such a terrible fate we had no idea when we five bold adventurers departed Fort Hanning early in April 1795.

My plan, as leader of our expedition, was to map the unexplored reaches of dense forest and wilderness around a mountain known to the natives as Aharihon, and since renamed Mt Darius, whose snow-capped peak dominates this untamed land.

We set out by following the Crowfoot River north, paddling our two canoes upstream, armed with musket and supplies, and making respectable progress for many weeks in this manner.

I had the greatest confidence in the four brave souls who accompanied me; my second in command was Luet Graves, who has had much experience exploring this savage land and a braver man I could not have hoped to meet.

George Tuller was our cartographer and, although not accustomed to the wilds, he acquitted himself well until his most tragic death, upon which I will elaborate soon.

The remaining two were twin brothers, Timothy and Josiah Dalderfield. They were our resident cooks and hunters both, although I swear that, despite their denials, they can have been no more than thirteen years of age at the outset of our adventure. Still, they were both fearless and resourceful to the bitter end, in spite of their youth.

We five journeyed for seven months, living off the land and enduring whatever obstacles Nature placed in our way: snowstorms, wild beasts, flash floods, freezing winds that slashed at our skin like a thousand cutlass blades. Yet, by the grace of the Almighty, we reached the foothills of Mt Darius late one afternoon in mid October.

"There be a lake of sorts ahead," young Josiah had informed us as he returned with a brace of waterfowl for our pot.

I shall never forget my first sight of that lake. Although I am not a superstitious man, looking upon that dead body of water, I felt that afternoon a ghastly premonition of something dark and evil. I sensed a lurking presence that watched our approach with baleful eyes.

The lake's water was black and frighteningly deep, like some ancient well filled with ominous secrets. Dead logs floated like bloated corpses on its dark surface. The lake itself, from what I could distinguish in the fading light, was heart-shaped, with a medium-sized island at its centre, densely wooded and inhospitable.

We made camp that night on the rocky foreshore, ate boiled waterfowl and succumbed to fitful sleep.

About midnight I was awoken by the sound of a canoe being dragged over the rocks to the lake.

I sprang to my feet and, in the moon's pale light, saw young Josiah standing by the lake edge, staring out over the black waters.

"'Tis Luet Graves, sir," said he. "He has taken the canoe and brother Timothy, both with muskets, out on the lake!"

"At this time of night? Why?" I demanded.

"Said he'd heard something, sir. A noise like. Thought it may be a beast of sorts."

"Beast? What kind of beast?"

"Maybe one of them alligators, sir."

We were joined then by George Tuller, who asserted that he, too, had heard a heavy splashing sound upon the water, and all three of us stood uncertainly, waiting for some sign from our companions.

Suddenly, there was the most blood-curdling scream I have ever heard or expect to hear! It sounded like the voice of Luet Graves, coming from the darkness of the lake, and it seemed to have been pulled from the very soul of that unfortunate man.

It was immediately followed by a musket shot and then the wail of young Timothy screaming, "My God! Have mercy!" His voice suddenly stopped dead, swallowed up in the sound of a frenzied thrashing of the waters. Then all was silent.

Stung to action, we three on the shore clambered

into the one remaining canoe and, with George holding a lamp aloft and me a loaded musket, Josiah paddled frantically out into that lake.

Of our friends we saw no sign, even though we filled the night with our shouting. After what seemed an eternity, yet was in actuality no more than an hour or so, young Josiah spied something on the outer edge of his lantern beam. "It be Luet Graves and his canoe!" he cried with delight.

Sure enough, the prow of a canoe drifted into view with what seemed to be Luet Graves seated upright in the bow. His hands, however, held no paddle; they hung limp over each side, trailing in the black water.

In eagerness, Josiah shouted out, "Sir! Have ye seen brother Timothy? Is he with ye?" But, as the canoe came more fully into the light, I saw the truth. Luet Graves was dead. His torso was upright, yet his lower body, from the waist down, was severed from it and lay akimbo, like some rag doll savaged by a wild dog.

The opposite side of the boat had been ripped in a most savage manner.

Reeling back at the horror of the sight, Josiah tipped our canoe most precipitously, sending George Tuller flailing into the maw of that black water. In vain I tried to right the canoe and pluck at his clothing in order to drag him back aboard. It seemed as if the lake had

5

swallowed him whole. Then, in a scene I will never be able to erase from my tormented memory, he arose out of the dreadful water! He was ensnared in the mouth of a creature so hideous I can barely describe it. With our companion in its jaws, limp like wet sailcloth, this vile creature exploded up out of the lake in the manner of a whale breaching. Yet it was no whale.

It had a serpentine body, black as sin itself, sleek and oily, pockmarked and pitted with scars. In size, I guessed it to be as long as a well-grown tree and as round at the girth as well. It bore some resemblance to a snake, with black eyes devoid of life, yet its massive mouth was toothed like that of a deep-sea fish. It looked, to my petrified eyes, like nothing less than some giant eel of a prehistoric origin.

I managed, I know not how, to unload one round from my musket into the face of this terrible beast. Its reaction was both swift and terrible.

Immediately dropping the very dead George Tuller from its now gaping mouth, it plunged again into the lake with a thunder of water that capsized the canoe, causing both Josiah and myself to tumble into the lake.

With my heart fit to explode, I swam in terror of that beast, thrashing for the safety of the shore of a nearby island.

To my eternal shame, I know nothing of Josiah's

final fate. Just once I heard him call my name in dread, somewhere on that cursed lake, then only silence.

I expected to be attacked at any moment: ripped asunder like my companions, dragged to some deep underwater lair.

For an instant, I felt the rub of something sleek and evil beneath my stomach as I swam those black waters. Yet, after half an hour of exhausting endeavour, I struck the slimy rocks that lined the shore of the lake's island.

Never have I been so grateful for the touch of dry land!

In spite of my exhausted state, I crawled up the shore, over the many razor-sharp rocks that lay strewn like broken glass, and up into the dense tree line. There I fell into a nightmarish sleep, with the screams of my friends and the sight of that hideous eel filling every corner of my dreams.

By the morning's light, I awoke and reviewed my pitiful situation.

I had sustained a fearsome number of wounds in my flight from the beast; a trail of blood could be seen leading up from the lake over the jagged rocks to where I now lay.

I had no canoe, no food and no musket. I was now master only of such things as I had on my person: a small knife, a sodden pouch of tobacco and my equally sodden journal and pen.

My chances of survival were meagre, I realised. Even if I could construct a raft of sorts and negotiate it back over that deadly lake, evading the evil creature's watchful eye, I would still be lost in a wilderness many months' journey from salvation. Our carefully drawn map now lay with my poor friend George Tuller at the bottom of the lake.

I spent a tormented day in agony, both from the impossibility of my position and from my many wounds. By week's end, I was weak with exhaustion, lack of food and loss of blood.

Now, gripped with a gangrenous fever, weak and at times delirious, I pen these words. Despite my pain, I know with startling clarity that I am dying and will never leave this island alive.

I therefore write these last words as testimony to my brave companions and also as a warning to whomever finds this journal.

PRAY BEWARE OF THE BLACK WATERS AND OF THE EVIL THAT RESIDES IN THIS LAKE OF THE DEAD!

Captain Ezra Bellevue, 1795

Chapter One

The only reason Josh Brookfield was still alive was that he'd never learned to tie a bowline.

His companions had laughed at his clumsiness. They could tie a bowline with their eyes shut. He'd watched as they all looped the rope about their waists and descended the cliff with ease, their laughter ringing in his ears. When the earthquake hit, their laughter stopped. He knew they were dead now, their bodies crushed beneath a mountain of rock below.

Earlier, when the first tremor had struck, they had all been badly shaken. Josh could see the panic in their eyes . . . smell the fear.

At first they had thought it must be thunder that

had shaken the ground so violently and they turned to peer at the westward sky. Great sheets of grey rain made visibility almost impossible. Only Mt Darius protruded above a landscape washed free of colour – slate grey and ominous.

"Sounded like thunder. Must be a storm heading this way!" Tom Packard had shouted above the strengthening wind.

At seventeen he was a year older than the rest and therefore considered himself to be the leader of the group.

It was not thunder. Josh had known that immediately.

The ground had begun to shake. He could barely stand straight, and had clutched at a tree branch to keep from plummeting forward. The ground seemed to roil and buckle under his feet.

Tom Packard staggered backwards then lurched dangerously close to the edge of the trail. Below them, a sheer drop plummeted 300 metres to a deep ravine scarred by a roaring river.

Greer Machon had screamed. The others in the group hadn't made a sound, but it wasn't due to bravery. They were simply shocked silent by pure, visceral fear.

Finally, the shaking stopped and silence fell, save

for the moaning of the wind.

They had all stumbled to their feet, stepping tentatively, as if they were walking on a trampoline, staring down into the misty ravine below.

"What on earth was that?" Matt Jablinski shouted, his freckled face turned white with fear. "That wasn't thunder!"

"Quake!" Greer had answered, her face also drained of colour.

"Quake? You mean, like an *earth*quake?" Matt turned to his twin brother Vinnie imploringly. "What do you think, Vin? Is she right?"

Vinnie simply nodded, his eyes unblinking in the driving rain.

They all stood silently on the trail, soaked and hunched, rain hoods pulled low across their faces, looking more like penitent monks on a dangerous pilgrimage than five high-school students on a hiking trip.

Their three-day hiking journey into the Bellevue Forest Wilderness to collect fossil samples had turned into a nightmare from the moment they'd stepped onto the trail.

Before they'd set out, Tom Packard, as usual, had placed himself in charge of checking the long-range weather forecast.

"Trust me. I know this place like the back of my hand. The weather's perfect this time of year."

Josh had had no reason to doubt him. After all, he hadn't been hiking in the Bellevue before. In fact, he hadn't been hiking *anywhere* before, a piece of information he had carefully forgotten to mention when he'd showed up at the Marantha High School Hiking Club meeting.

The other four in the group were all experienced in the outdoors and had welcomed a newcomer in their midst. Marantha High was a sporty school and football and athletics dominated. Only the Chess Club rated below the Hiking Club in popularity.

The Hiking Club members had gabbed on all through the meeting about the joys of the trail and debated the pros and cons of an assortment of camping equipment Josh had never even seen before, never mind knowing what any of it was for! But he had managed to nod sagely and keep his mouth shut.

Truth was, he hated the thought of hiking. The idea of spending three days in the wilderness, wearing a bulging backpack and silly-looking boots, repulsed him. Give him three days on the sofa with a remote control and enough chips to choke an elephant and he couldn't be happier. He had joined the Hiking Club for an entirely different reason.

Only Tom Packard seemed to suspect his motives. Not that he said anything to Josh. It was just the sideways looks he gave him and the thin smile that never reached his eyes.

The club had chosen the Bellevue Forest for their mid-term hike and preparations were in full swing. Josh had barely heard of it – a wilderness of over a hundred thousand hectares, more than eight hours' drive to the north.

On the first morning, they had arrived at the car park of the Bellevue Ranger Station and poured out of the bus. Tom Packard had blithely dismissed Josh's concern at gathering black clouds on the horizon. "Passing shower, nothing more." Then he'd winked at Josh and grinned maliciously. "But I'm sure you know that, Brookfield, with all your hiking experience."

Josh hadn't answered. He'd slung his pack and fallen in behind the others, listening to snatches of their conversations.

Matt and Vinnie were arguing vehemently in a brotherly way about whether or not you could survive by drinking your own urine if nothing else was available.

"Too salty!" Matt had declared.

"How d'you know? Drunk some recently?" Vinnie had replied, thumping him on the shoulder and laughing wickedly.

Greer was up front with Packard, deep in conversation about different types of rock strata. Josh heard him trying to impress her by spouting some rubbish about "toroweap sandstone deposits and kaibab limestone".

"Loser!" Josh had thought.

That's when it had begun to rain. And rain hard.

The forecast Packard had so confidently passed on – a fine spell of cool autumn weather – rapidly turned into a three-day rainstorm of biblical intensity. Sheets of unrelenting rain had swept the bleak landscape, soaking it, and them, within minutes.

They had staggered to their first campsite, sodden, cold and cheerless.

After a sleepless night in wet sleeping bags and saturated tents, the new day revealed a sky of lead and a continuing torrent of rain.

Packard had desperately tried to locate an alternative place to shelter on the map. "I know of a hunter's cabin up the Crowfoot River . . . about nineteen kilometres off the trail. It'll be dry and we could be there by nightfall."

Josh would rather have just turned back to the car park. With cold rain pouring down his back like a waterfall and blisters the size of golf balls on every part of his feet, he cursed himself repeatedly for ever having stepped into this stupid forest.

Yet he hadn't wanted to be a wimp, especially when Greer had stoically shouldered her pack and followed Packard's lead.

After a miserable day of trudging through blinding rain and mud, they had arrived exhausted, cold and hungry at the hunter's cabin, only to discover that it was no more than a pile of charred timber, burned to the ground long ago.

No one had said anything – they'd been too exhausted to speak, too disappointed for words.

That second night was spent shivering under the dripping canopy of a fir tree, eating cold pumpkin soup from a shared can. A fire had been impossible in the sleeting rain and strong wind. Anyway, all their matches, along with everything else, were nothing more than a sodden lump in the bottom of their saturated packs.

"I've survived worse!" Packard boasted. "This is nothing!"

Josh had wanted to punch his lights out.

The next morning had dawned even colder

and greyer, and the rain of the previous night had intensified, if such a thing were possible. Rivers of water flooded over the sodden ground, ankle-deep and rising.

"We'll have to turn back," Josh had finally ventured.

Packard turned on him angrily.

"Turn back? Who put you in charge, Brookfield? I say we keep on going . . . try to pick up the trail and head for the Darius Crossing."

Greer's eyes had widened at that.

"Darius Crossing? But, Tom, that'll take us to the foot of Mt Darius . . . that's miles from our planned route."

Packard brushed her comment aside.

"I'm changing the planned route! Okay? We head for higher ground and wait out this storm . . . it'll pass. Trust me, Darius Crossing is our best, our *only*, option."

He began to fold the map, ending the discussion, yet Josh had seen fear dancing in his eyes.

He'd spoken up. "It was hard enough following that trail yesterday. Now, with all this rain, it'll be completely washed out, won't it?" He thrust a finger at the sodden map. "Didn't I see a dam to the west? Why don't we try for that? Looks like a group of buildings on the map. There's sure to be someone there and guaranteed to be shelter . . ."

Tom Packard had turned on him like a cornered animal, angrily wiping the rain from his eyes.

"That's the Wicker Dam, you idiot! It's been abandoned for more than a hundred years! There's nothing there but more water!" He hastily finished folding the map and stuffed it back in his pack, then added angrily, "Anyway, what do you know about anything? You've never hiked a mile in your sorry life before now." He leaned in close to Josh's face – so close Josh could smell the warm stench of his breath – and hissed, "We all know the *real* reason you wanted to tag along, Brookfield." He had looked in Greer's direction, a sneer forming on his lips. "You didn't want to miss the stunning scenery, did you, fat boy?"

Then, with a dismissive wave, he strode off up the muddy trail, calling over his shoulder, "So, if no one else has got any bright ideas, we might just make it to Darius Crossing before dark!"

Matt and Vinnie had obediently slung their packs and trudged after him, leaving Josh under the tree, his face burning red under his soaking hood.

Greer had lingered a moment, adjusting the straps on her pack. Then she had suddenly turned to him, brushing wet hair from her face.

"For what it's worth, Josh, I agree with you. The Wicker would've been a good option."

He had looked up startled; it was the first time Greer had ever talked to him directly.

"Then why didn't you say something?" he asked.

She stood with her fingers looped through her pack straps, looking at Josh uncertainly.

They were classmates at Marantha, had been for four years, yet she hardly knew Josh Brookfield. In fact, this conversation was longer than any she'd had with him in all that time. Josh kept to himself – he wasn't a team player. He was the kind of guy who lurked around the edges of life, rather than participating in it. It wasn't that he was unpopular or anything; nor was he the target of any bullying. His size was enough to put any potential bully off. She'd heard a few people call him Bear, and that pretty much summed Josh up. He was big for his age, craggy, with a slight stoop of the shoulders and a loping way of walking. He was the type who let the river of life slide right on past while he lolled on the bank watching.

Greer, on the other hand, plunged right in. She soaked herself in all that life brought her way. She was popular and confident with it. Brainy, absolutely, but in a way you applauded not resented. Their two orbits were not in alignment.

Until now.

He had felt her eyes boring into him and shouldered his wet pack awkwardly.

She thinks I'm an idiot, he thought, a dumb bear. They all do.

"It doesn't matter anyway," he said. "Packard's right. The dam sounds like it's abandoned." He'd begun hiking up the trail. "I've never actually been there – never been *anywhere* out here, for that matter . . . so what would I know about the dam or anything."

Greer had followed after him. "The dam was constructed in 1900, named after some rich guy, Samuel Z Wicker III. It was supposed to generate enough power to light up a new city he'd named Metropolene. They built the dam, but not the city . . . old Samuel Z went bankrupt."

Josh turned slightly and peered back at her around the rim of his dripping hood. She *was* a smart cookie. And drop-dead gorgeous with it! For four years he'd watched her over the edge of his textbooks or from the sidelines. All the guys had.

He smiled, in spite of the rain that now flowed freely down the inside of his shirt. She caught his smile and suddenly her green eyes flashed angrily.

"You think I'm some sort of walking Google, don't you? Give Greer a subject, any subject, and her search-engine brain will give you all the answers!" She had pushed on by him, almost knocking him into the trees at the side of the trail.

Through the rain he had watched her catch up with the others.

"Smart, gorgeous *and* fiery!" he thought.

They had hiked all day through ankle-deep mud, with Packard incessantly urging them on in the driving rain. To make matters worse, a freezing cold wind was whipping up off the mountain.

It was late afternoon by then, bleak and getting dark, and still no sign of the trail to Darius Crossing. Yet on and on they had stumbled, chins on chests, like a chain gang, blindly following the leader.

Suddenly, Josh had had enough. He slumped exhausted into the mud and rested his aching back against a wet tree trunk.

Packard's harsh voice whipped through the rain. "Get up, Brookfield! I'm sick of hauling you over these mountains! If we keep having to babysit you, we're never going to get to Darius Crossing!"

To everyone's surprise, Josh had dropped his pack and jumped to his feet, eyes blazing, pushing past the others to where Packard stood.

"Darius Crossing?" He spat the words out. "Why don't you tell them, Packard? Tell them the truth about Darius Crossing!"

Packard had stepped back, momentarily stunned by Josh's sudden outburst. Then he'd grabbed Josh by the front of his raincoat, thrusting his face into Josh's.

"Tell them *what,* Brookfield?"

Josh pulled free and jabbed a finger in his chest.

"Tell them that you're lost! *Lost!* Have been for hours! Tell them that!"

Packard's face drained of colour. "Lost? Are you crazy? What makes you think that I'm lost?" he shouted, spittle forming in the corner of his mouth. "I know exactly where we are . . . Do *you,* Brookfield?"

Josh turned to him. "No, I haven't got a clue where we are . . . Neither do you. And *this* is why!"

He pointed at a tree trunk by the path. The letters JB were crudely carved in the wood.

Greer had stepped forward then. "What's got into you, Josh?"

He turned to face her and the others. "I carved those letters in that tree hours ago, when we stopped for a break . . . Packard's been leading us around in circles!"

Josh whirled to confront him again. "So, you tell them, *Tom*. Tell them you're *lost*!"

That was when the first tremor hit.

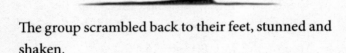

The group scrambled back to their feet, stunned and shaken.

"What on earth was that?" Matt had shouted. "That wasn't thunder!"

"Quake!" Greer had answered.

"Quake? You mean, like an *earth*quake?" Matt had turned to his brother. "What do you think, Vin? Is she right?"

And Vinnie had remained silent, his eyes unblinking in the driving rain.

"That was definitely a quake," Greer said, her eyes wide with fear, the wind whipping her wet hair free of her rain hood.

She turned to Packard, who was mutely staring out over the rain-lashed treetops toward Mt Darius. "Are we really lost, Tom?"

He didn't answer her, just stood staring at the mountain. They followed his catatonic gaze.

Mt Darius rose majestically from the grey landscape, its snow-capped peak thrusting up to the leaden thunderclouds above.

But it wasn't the mountain that caught their attention. It was the huge plume of black smoke that had begun billowing out from its crater top.

Again, Greer broke the silence. "It's going to erupt, isn't it?" she cried above the wind. "That quake was from the mountain!"

Packard still said nothing, his arms limp at his side, but he nodded imperceptibly.

Matt grabbed him by the arm, swinging him bodily around to face him, panic in his voice. His words spilled out in a jumble.

"Erupt? It can't . . . can it? I mean, it's supposed to be a dead volcano, right? Tom? It's dead . . ."

Packard was still staring at Mt Darius, his mouth moving open and shut like a mountain trout.

Josh answered for him. "It's obviously not *dead any more.* That quake means that it's coming back to life."

"Then we've got to get out of here . . . now!" shouted Matt, shouldering his pack and stumbling off down the trail, back in the direction they'd just come. "Come on, Vinnie! Let's get out of here!"

Greer turned uncertainly and began to follow, leaving Josh and Packard still standing on the edge of the trail, transfixed by the billowing clouds rising from the caldera on Mt Darius.

Josh tore his eyes away and turned to shout after them, "Where exactly are you all headed? We're lost . . . remember?"

"Maybe! But I'm getting as far away from that mountain as I can!" Matt shouted back, pointing to the ravine below. "There's a river down below. Must be the Crowfoot. If we follow it downstream, it'll lead us back out!"

The steep sides of the ravine were covered with a dangerous-looking slip of loose shingle. A long way down, the river was a slash of silver in the mist.

"How are you going to get *down* there?" Josh asked incredulously, his words lost in the wind.

Suddenly, Packard snapped back to life. Pushing past Josh, he strode down the trail towards the others.

"We'll use the ropes!" he cried, with unnerving enthusiasm. His eyes blazed with a kind of mad fervour.

Eager to follow a plan, any plan, the rest of the group hurriedly opened their packs and began retrieving an assortment of ropes.

Packard hastily knotted the hotchpotch of ropes together to form a substantial length and looped one end around a sturdy fir tree growing on the ravine's edge.

"Each of you in turn will tie a bowline around your waist and abseil down the ravine. The next in line pulls up the rope. Hurry!"

Matt went first, tying the rope around his waist and lowering himself awkwardly over the lip of the trail and down into the sheer ravine. After a tense moment when he caused a minor landslide of rubble with his flailing feet, he reached the ravine floor amid a small avalanche of rock. Viewed from the trail above, he was a tiny, forlorn figure with the rain pelting down around him.

"I'm down!" he shouted up, untying the rope. "Pull it up!"

Packard hauled the rope swiftly up the slope.

Vinnie went next, swiftly tying a bowline around his waist, gangly legs kicking out over the ravine, accompanied by showers of shingle.

In the distance, Mt Darius was still belching smoke.

Greer hesitated before taking her turn. "What about you, Tom?"

"Don't worry. I'll go last."

She threw a last anxious look at Josh, then disappeared over the edge.

Packard hauled the rope back up but, instead of handing it to Josh, he tied it around his own waist.

"If you hadn't got us lost, we wouldn't have to be doing this," Josh hissed.

Packard's eyes flared and the smile he gave Josh was one of pure malevolence. "Maybe. But now you've got to get your lazy self down this ravine because Greer ain't here to help you . . . Sure hope you know how to tie a bowline, fat boy!"

Then, with a sick laugh, he slid over the side and rappelled expertly down the shingle slope to the others. Soon, the four of them were standing in the driving rain, staring up at Josh as he pulled in the wet rope and wiped the rain out of his eyes.

Truth was he had no idea how to knot a bowline. He looped the rope around his waist and fumbled with the end, attempting the knot he'd seen the others tie so effortlessly. But they could obviously tie a bowline in their sleep! He had trouble tying his own school tie.

When he had a knot that resembled a bowline, he gingerly began to lower himself over the ledge. Almost immediately, the wet knot untangled itself, leaving him dangling precariously, clutching the end of the rope.

He could hear Matt's voice calling from below. "Come on, Josh. We've got to make tracks before this whole place goes up!"

Now he heard Packard snigger. "Fat boy can't even tie his own shoelaces!"

Josh's gut was churning in panic. His hands shook as he attempted to tie the knot again. It was like trying to tie wet spaghetti!

The wind had a cruel knife-edge to it now and the rain was sleeting almost horizontally, stinging his eyes as he desperately tried to focus.

"Tie the rope, Brookfield, and get on with it!" shouted Packard.

He heard Greer ask, "Why didn't you let him go before you, Tom? Does he know how to tie a bowline?"

"How should I know? Fat boy knows everything, doesn't he?" Packard's sneering voice floated up with a fierce gust of wind.

Josh's face flushed red. His heart was pounding fit to burst. Was it left over right or right over left? His hands were like frozen lumps, fingers thick with cold. As he attempted one more loop, the slippery rope suddenly slid through his hands and snaked away down the slope, where it was greeted with moans by the others.

Greer leapt forward and looped the rope around her waist.

Josh could hear Packard's frantic voice. "What are you doing?"

"He obviously *can't* tie a bowline, no thanks to you. I'm going back up to help him!"

Before Packard could protest, she was calling up to Josh. "Pull me up!"

Humiliated beyond words, Josh hauled with all his strength, praying that the knots linking the rope together would hold. When Greer's determined face appeared over the ledge, he wished Mt Darius would explode and bury him in his embarrassment.

She deflected his mumbled apology, looping the rope around his waist.

"No time for that. Let's get back down before . . ."

Her words were lost in a deafening wall of noise that sucked the air from their lungs – a terrifying roar, drawn from the bowels of the earth. After a thousand years of slumber, Mt Darius had awoken. Awoken with a vengeance.

White-hot magma, racing upwards from the Earth's tortured core, was pouring into the volcanic cone, blasting through the crust and erupting with violent fury. A fearsome mushroom cloud of molten rock and ash exploded from the crater. It raced skyward, then spread with astonishing speed over the Bellevue Forest, blotting out the sunlight.

The ground convulsed, tossing the group of stunned hikers in the ravine off their feet and smashing them into trees and boulders, pummelling them with a wave of soil and rock that lifted them high on its crest, only to dump them down again with bone-breaking force.

Josh grabbed at the rope and clung on for dear life. Tonnes of debris pounded down around him. A rock smacked the side of his head and his vision blurred red.

He was aware of Greer crashing into him, felt a boot in his face, a landslide of smothering soil tumbling them over and over. For hours, the destruction continued unabated. The sky was black with vomited ash, the forest ablaze with fire.

Josh's world was reduced to a choking blackness and an eerie silence, buried beneath a landslide of wet soil and rubble. He felt as if he was in a deep black-water hole, the kind he had swum in as a kid, and he was being tugged inexorably down by the current. Down to his death . . . the air slowly strangled from his lungs . . .

Night crept over the Bellevue. The fire still raged, lighting the dark sky in a scene from hell itself.

During the night, a series of violent aftershocks rolled over the forest. It was one of these that shook the soil free from Josh's face, exposing it to the cold night air.

At last the descent into black water was over and he was swimming back to the surface. He burst into full consciousness with a gasp for air, frantically clawing his way out of the wet soil and tangled branches that enveloped him.

His waist felt as if it was almost cut in two, and he realised that the rope Greer had tied around him was still miraculously tied to the fir tree. Frantically, he pulled on it and, like a mole emerging from hibernation, broke free of his soil tomb.

A scene from a nightmare greeted him. Flames lit the night sky, revealing huge clouds of ash above him. The whole side of the ravine above the Crowfoot River had disappeared in an avalanche of shingle and mud, completely obliterating the valley and the river below. There was no sign of Packard, Matt or Vinnie. The spot they had stood on was now covered in tonnes of debris.

All that had saved him from a similar fate was the rope, still tied to what remained of the tree, snapped in half by the force of the avalanche.

Painfully, he hauled himself up, calling out Greer's name, blood flowing freely into his eyes from a jagged gash in his head.

To his stunned amazement, she answered almost immediately.

He found her wrapped around the same tree that had saved his own life. A pile of soil and shingle had encased her up to the waist and would have swept her to her death had it not been for the tree. Blood flowed from her nose and mud plastered her face, with just the whites of her eyes showing through, but she was alive. He clawed at the soil around her with his bare hands.

Together, they scrambled up the side of the landslide and sat crouched and dazed in the lee of a fallen tree, surveying the scene before them.

Mt Darius was no more. Its entire eastern side had collapsed like a rotten molar, black volcanic ash spiralling from the gaping hole.

Bellevue, too, was no more. Everywhere, trees lay uprooted and scattered, hurled to the ground and burning like a hundred thousand blackened matchsticks.

Lake Of The Dead

They could find no words to speak. So they just held each other, exhausted and in a state of shock, and waited for morning.

Chapter Two

The dead deer was beginning to bloat, causing its legs to stick straight out from its body.

Josh approached it cautiously, as if it might suddenly leap up and bound away.

"Looks like it's been dead for a day or two," Greer said, as she stepped past him to examine the carcass.

Josh wrinkled his nose at the smell and tried to think of something intelligent to say.

"Must've died in the eruption," was all he could manage, and kicked himself when he saw her roll her eyes.

"Do you reckon the meat will still be okay?" he added.

They hadn't eaten anything in more than forty-eight hours and this was the first edible thing they'd stumbled on.

In the aftermath of the eruption they had cowered together beneath the remains of the tree stump that had saved their lives. All night the ground trembled as they shivered with shock and fear. They hadn't heard a sound from their companions, though Greer had shouted herself hoarse calling out their names.

Josh knew they were never going to answer.

He had attempted to clamber down the steep shingle landslide to the bottom of the ravine, but only succeeded in causing an avalanche of debris and rocks that sucked and pulled at his feet.

Retreating back to the shelter of the tree, he knew full well that Packard, Matt and Vinnie could never have survived the rock fall and were buried together beneath a small mountain of boulders. Forever.

That wasn't the only truth they had had to face when morning arrived, grey and dismal. The realisation of the deadly predicament they were in hit them hard as well.

It was Greer who had summed up their situation. "We've got no water, our packs and supplies are gone and Tom had the only map. We can't stay here;

it's too dangerous. Mt Darius could erupt again at any moment. Best to head west towards the Wicker Dam. There might be someone still there or a telephone or something."

"Why move at all?" Josh asked. "The authorities will be swarming over the Bellevue once news of the eruption gets out. They'll send in a chopper for sure."

She pointed at the devastated landscape around them. "Take a look, Josh. There *is* no more Bellevue, at least nothing recognisable. It'd be like looking for a needle in a haystack. The eruption has flattened almost everything and the rest is on fire. With all that smoke and ash in the sky, not even a sparrow's going to be flying for days."

As if on cue, the sky seemed to drop around them in a choking cloud of smoke and ash, taking visibility down to virtually nil.

In this grim netherworld of mist they had set out, heading west as best as Greer could determine.

For two days they struggled and stumbled through a moonscape of destruction. The Bellevue Forest had been levelled by the eruption and Mt Darius, visible from time to time through the ash clouds, still smoked ominously above the devastation. They passed blackened trees and land-slides of rubble, all enveloped by grey volcanic ash and reeking with the rotten-egg stench of sulphur.

Greer kept repeating, "I don't recognise any of this! Everything has changed." Still, whenever the sun's weak glow managed to break through the choking clouds, she was able to correct their course in a westerly direction.

They were weary beyond words by the afternoon of the second day. Their lips were cracked with thirst and their entire bodies caked in grey, clinging ash. Blood still seeped from Josh's head wound. And now hunger gnawed at their guts.

Things were looking hopeless and the light, already gloomy because of the ash cloud, was beginning to fade. Josh felt ready to crumple in a heap and simply give up. And that's when they'd stumbled over a ridge into the valley below and spotted the dead deer.

Greer inspected the animal, poking it with her finger. It was a hind, its cold eyes fixed wide open in death. Ash covered most of the body but, apart from the smell, it seemed as though it could be reasonably edible. Anyway they were both starving.

"I think it'll be all right," she said. "Once we cook it."

"Cook it?" Josh was so hungry, he'd have eaten it raw.

"Yeah, we'll need to butcher it first and then cook the meat over a fire."

"Butcher it? Over a fire?" he repeated.

Greer stood up and eyeballed him. "You sound like my granny's parrot." Then, while Josh felt his cheeks turn every shade of red possible, she reached into the side pocket of her torn camo pants and pulled out a small pocket-knife.

"We'll need to carve it with this; it's all I've got. Ever butchered an animal before?"

He was about to say "butchered an animal before?" but didn't want to sound like her granny's parrot again. So he took the knife.

"I saw my uncle butcher a sheep once."

"Same thing, I suppose. Where do you think you'll start?"

"I said I'd only *seen* my uncle do it . . . I've never actually butchered a . . ."

"Listen to me, Josh!" she interrupted, eyes fiery. "We *need* to eat, because one more day out here without food and we'll end up as dead as this deer! So, whether you've only *seen* your uncle do it, or whether you've never butchered anything before, it doesn't matter! *Please*, just try, Josh, just try. . ."

Suddenly, her face seemed to melt. Tears spilled from her eyes and ran down her grimy face. She slumped to her knees and began to sob – deep, gut-wrenching sobs that seemed to come from deep inside her. She kept repeating the word "please" in between her sobs.

Josh didn't have a clue what he should do. He remembered finding his mother sobbing over the kitchen sink one day when he returned home from school early. It was around the time of his father's death. He hadn't known what to do then, either – how to comfort her. So he'd silently gone to his room and shut the door.

Greer's sobbing faded to a soft whimper. He knew she was exhausted, drained; they both were at the very end of their tethers. His impulse was to embrace her, comfort her somehow, and tell her it was going to be okay. He took an awkward step towards her hunched figure, unsure what to do or say. He reached out, but his outstretched arm froze in mid-air.

Maybe actions would speak louder than words, he thought. So he unclasped the knife blade instead and stepped over to the carcass of the deer.

He could feel her eyes on him as he hesitated, unsure where to begin. The last thing he wanted was to stuff this up by showing her what a complete klutz he was.

So, propelled by equal amounts of bravado and sheer hunger, he grasped the deer's back leg and began to hack away at the hindquarters.

The blade was small and blunt but, after half an hour of exertion, his hands and forearms sticky with blood and gore, he had somehow managed to separate a sizeable chunk of hindquarter. It wasn't pretty, but he was proud of his effort. He looked around to see if Greer was still watching.

For a chilling moment he realised she was no longer with him, but a moment later she appeared with a few bits of scorched firewood, returning at intervals to check his progress before announcing she was off to look for embers. Many of the burned trees they had passed earlier were still smoking from the eruption, and the embers had been smouldering with a soft red glow.

Josh stood up with the hind's bloody leg dangling from his hand. When Greer was gone, he suddenly felt very alone. All around him was destruction and death, low clouds of grey ash pressed in above him. His home, his family were . . . who knew how many days away. Would they find him dead like the hind, bloated and stinking, eyes fixed open in death?

Greer's voice broke through his morbid thoughts. "Josh! *Josh!* I've got fire!"

She had appeared over the grey ridge, her hands cupped around a few precious lumps of glowing ember, protected by a piece of bark.

Quickly, Josh assembled a semi-circle of rocks and piled a handful of firewood in the centre, the way he'd seen them do in the movies.

Greer lowered the piece of bark with its cargo of embers into the middle of the sticks and began to blow gently. The dull red lumps glowed into life with every puff and then, wondrously, burst into flame.

Josh thought he'd never seen such a welcome sight in his life. They both laughed with pure delight at the sight of those dancing flames.

With a large, sharpened stick, Josh speared the hindquarters and was about to place the meat on the fire when Greer stopped him.

"I think we should wash all the ash and stuff off first."

He looked at her, confused. "We haven't seen any clean water in days, Greer."

It was true. The only water they had seen was small, undrinkable puddles thick with silt and ash.

She beckoned him from the fire. "Come on. Bring the meat. There's something I want to show you."

He trailed after her, carrying the hindquarters, up a steep slope then down through a thicket of blackened trees. The grey afternoon light was fading fast, and Josh, struggling over uneven rocks, could barely make out what lay ahead.

Suddenly, his feet splashed into cold water. He dropped to his knees in amazement, drenching himself to the waist.

"It's a lake, Josh!" Greer cried. "I found it while I was getting the firewood."

They stood knee-deep and splashed each other joyously for a moment. Then they washed the meat and themselves and returned up the slope to the fire, happily wet and ravenously hungry.

Soon the night air was filled with the spit and fizzle of roasting meat. They dined like kings, hungrily tearing hunks of blackened meat off the bone and stuffing it into their mouths, fingers and chins glistening with grease.

Then, with the fire stoked and their stomachs bloated, they slept dreamlessly in the flickering firelight, like two exhausted dogs.

Josh was awoken the next morning by the sound of

splashing. He prised open his eyes, still thick with sleep, and squinted around him. The fire was dark and cold, just burned bone and ash. Sunlight seeped through a sky hanging like a dirty sheet. He shivered and stretched painfully.

Then the realisation hit him. Greer was gone.

Josh stumbled urgently towards the lake, following the sound of splashing, calling out Greer's name. The foreshore was draped in mist and he tripped painfully on the slimy rocks as he scrambled to the water's edge.

"Greer! Is that you?"

In the dim, filtered sunlight he scanned the lake. It was, as best he could tell, about two kilometres wide, its waters deep and dark, almost pitch-black in places. The shoreline pressed in all around, its dank foliage clawing at the water's edge. The surface was covered in floating debris, rotten tree stumps mostly, with broken branches reaching out of the water like a drowning man's hands. Hanks of mist drifted between them, giving it the look of some spectral, watery graveyard.

Josh shivered. It was not just the cold. Something about the lake seemed ancient and sinister.

Then he spied Greer.

She was floating on her back, eyes closed, as

motionless as the half-submerged logs, arms and legs spread wide, drifting in some unseen current.

He waded into the lake, shouting her name, praying she was alive.

Suddenly, she kicked her feet, correcting her course, and he realised that she was just floating on her back. Feeling like an idiot, he hoped she hadn't heard the panic in his voice.

She hadn't. Her head was partially submerged, ears covered, eyes closed, calmly drifting in a pool of weak morning sun. She was unaware that Josh was staring at her. Gaping actually. In the yellow light that dappled the dark water, with the grime and ash washed from her face and her black hair spread like spilled ink about her, Josh thought she looked . . . radiant.

He watched her quietly for a long time until he realised that her eyes were open and she was staring back at him. Flushing red, he began scanning the lake, as if he had just arrived at the water's edge and was searching for her amid the floating logs.

"How long have you been standing there?" she called out, still floating on her back. But, before he could mumble a reply, she added, "I was hoping you'd wake up sooner or later. Come on in, there's something I want to show you."

Josh hesitated. The lake was icy and deep.

But he could feel her eyes on him. So, stumbling over the uneven rocks, pushing aside his fears, he dived in and immediately felt the cold water tear at his bare skin. Surging to the surface, he gasped with the sheer shock of it.

"Cold, huh?" she said, gurgling with laughter. "You'll warm up once you start swimming."

And with that she rolled onto her stomach and began swimming off through the mist towards the middle of the lake.

Josh plunged after her. He wasn't a great swimmer. His arms splashed clumsily in the black water and he kept bumping into dead logs, but the movement warmed him considerably.

Every few metres, he trod water to catch his breath and look for Greer, who was powering further away from him, stroke by stroke.

The mist seemed to be enveloping her now. Where on earth was she going? What did she want to show him in the middle of the lake?

He grappled for a floating log, hugging it as it rolled away from him. His heart pounded with the exertion as he peered across the misty surface of the lake, looking for her. By now he had swum further than he'd ever swum before and he was exhausted, his arms and legs knotting painfully with cramp.

The mist had thickened, blotting out what little sunlight there had been. It swirled around him now, leaving him clutching at his rotten log like a shipwrecked sailor in a sea of fog.

That's when he sensed it. An icy cold finger of fear touched his heart. It was a feeling of something watching him . . . not from the shore, but from the deep, below his churning legs.

He felt panic rising up within him and the cold realisation of where he was struck him. He was in the middle of an unknown lake, and the water below was ominously black and terrifyingly deep. Something was down there, something menacing, something that meant him harm. He kicked hard in a frenzy, desperately looking around for Greer. Where was she? The mist was thick, swirling about him like a wet sheet. His whole body shivered uncontrollably now, making it almost impossible to keep his grip on the bobbing log as he thrashed through the dark water.

He felt the log sliding away from him as his numb fingers frantically clawed at its slippery surface. Then it was gone and he was slipping back into the lake, floundering hopelessly in the cold water, pounding at it with his hands, gulping mouthfuls as his head slid under the surface, choking, sinking . . .

Suddenly, he felt an arm around him, pulling him to the surface. It was Greer.

He broke back through the surface of the water, gasping for air as she guided him to a log and helped haul him over it.

He lay slumped, his legs trailing in the water, his chest heaving painfully.

"You all right?"

He could hear the panic in her voice.

"I shouldn't have swum on ahead like that. I should have asked you if you could swim . . . I'm sorry, Josh."

They drifted for a while in silence, Greer in the water guiding the log with her feet. When he had regained his breath, he spoke without looking back at her.

"Thanks."

"Don't thank me. It was my fault . . . I just wanted to show you the island."

"Island?" He was incredulous. He had almost drowned because she wanted to show him an island?

"There are buildings on it," she said. "Maybe a town."

"Buildings? A town? Where?" The words were out before he could stop them. Granny's parrot.

She pointed across the dark waters. "Over there. Do you see it?"

He peered across the dark lake. The mist still hung low on the water but, rising above it, he could clearly make out the silhouette of an island. Its shoreline was crowded with lifeless trees, bare and jagged like rows of broken teeth. But beyond, Josh could make out something else, something man-made . . . the distinct shape of buildings and rooftops.

"What is this place?" he asked, but Greer was already kicking away from the log and swimming to the island. "Only one way to find out. Stay with the log, Josh. Use it like a canoe . . ."

He watched her swim through the mist, momentarily losing sight of her. Then he saw her figure emerge and stumble up the rocky shore, turning to call back to him.

"There's some sort of jetty over here!"

He began to paddle towards her, slumped over the log as if on a surfboard, kicking with his feet. The mist was moving in again like a living thing, wet and thick. He paddled faster, hoping to break through it at any moment and reach Greer.

"Josh!" he heard her call. "*Josh!*" There was urgency in her voice, bordering on panic.

"I'm coming!" he shouted back. "It's this mist! How far . . ."

Suddenly, Greer's scream pierced the air.

"Greer! What's wrong?" he shouted, paddling ferociously now, blinded by the mist.

"Josh! Get out of the water! *Now!*" she cried.

Cold panic gripped his heart. "What is it . . . what's happening?"

"There's something . . . something in the water!"

He whirled around, desperately scanning the black water, but all he could see was the roiling mist.

"Get out of the water, Josh!"

Suddenly, the log was hit from beneath with a violent impact that threw Josh backwards into the water. His legs struck something hard and unforgiving and panic overtook him. He surged for the surface, flailing at the water in blind terror, and found that, miraculously, he had somehow reached the rocky fringe of the island. He hauled himself out of the water, stumbled up the steep foreshore and dropped to his knees, gasping for breath and frantically looking for Greer.

She was no more than a metre away, standing higher up the rocky shore as if carved from granite, her arm outstretched, hand pointing. Her mouth was open but no words came out; her terrified eyes were fixed on something behind Josh's head, back towards the lake.

He turned anxiously to look where she was pointing. The log he'd paddled was bumping against the shore, mist hung low on the water and beyond that the lake lurked dark and deep.

His chest heaving as he gasped for air, Josh was about to ask her what she had seen when, as if in slow motion, he saw it for himself. There was something in the water. Something huge.

Josh stood transfixed. At first he thought it must be a snake of some sort, yet the sheer size of it stunned him. It was black in colour, easily the length of a fallen tree, maybe ten metres end to end, and at least as thick about its girth as a man . . . a very large man. As the black creature began rising swiftly from the depths of the lake, moving with sinister, serpentine speed, he saw it was longer than he had thought, much like an eel . . . a giant eel!

Suddenly, it broke the surface, its great head bursting out of the water to reveal lifeless eyes of pitch-black and a gaping slash of a mouth lined with rows of fishhook-sharp teeth.

Greer screamed, over and over – an hysterical chant – and Josh staggered backwards up the rocky shore towards her, unable to tear his eyes from the hideous sight.

The creature sat completely still in the water, its head raised above the surface, and Josh realised, in a sickening moment of dread, that it was watching them with its dead eyes.

Then, just as suddenly as it had appeared, it slid back beneath the dark waters and was gone.

Chapter Three

There might have been a thriving town there on the island in the middle of the black lake. Perhaps even a handsome town, with paved streets and brick buildings lining the walkways.

Maybe once.

But not any more.

As Greer and Josh approached, still in shock from their encounter with the creature, it was obvious that no one had lived there for a very long time.

The place was a ghost town. Derelict buildings squatted in the mist like drunken old men, leaning against each other for support. The whole place reeked of death and decay, a putrefying rottenness.

Cautiously, Greer stepped over the blackened

logs that lay in the middle of what had once been a main street. Now it was no more than a strip of mud littered with rotten debris. Fallen bricks lay in discarded heaps everywhere, as if smashed by a giant fist and scattered in anger. Doorways gaped black and empty, and glassless windows stared out from shattered frames.

"This place is dead," Greer whispered, as if afraid to wake the ghosts of the past.

"Been dead for a while, I'd say," Josh answered. "Got any idea where we are?"

She looked around, trying to get a bearing. The town and the island were crouched in the middle of a large, heart-shaped lake, surrounded on all sides by the remains of a steeply sloped forest. Massive landslides had transformed the landscape and, beyond the hilltops, she could see nothing but low-lying clouds of ash.

"I don't recognise this place at all. This town's not on any map I've ever seen, let alone this island or the lake we swam across."

The thought of having swum the lake with that creature lurking below made them both shiver and stare back towards the cold, dark water.

"What on earth was that thing?" asked Josh.

Greer's face was still drawn and white and, when

she failed to answer, Josh filled the silence.

"Looked like some sort of giant eel. Did you see the size of it? My brothers and I used to spear eels down by the creek at the back of our place. They were big, slippery creatures – nasty, too. But I've never seen one that size . . . ever! It was looking at us, Greer . . . I mean really looking at us, as if. . ."

"Shut up, Josh!"

He was stunned.

"I was only . . ."

"Shut up! Please, Josh." There was pleading in her voice, but her eyes flickered with fury.

They sat on a pile of bricks, not talking for a long time. The vision of that giant eel, its dead eyes staring at them, filled their thoughts. They both knew the truth. There was no help or rescue to be found in this ghost town. That meant they would need to leave the island. And the only way back was the way they had come . . . across the lake.

Even if they could make it back to the other side, where should they go from there? Where were they?

Finally, Josh spoke out loud. "We've been heading west for two days now, right?"

She looked up at the watery sun, glad of a change of subject.

"Sure. As best as I can tell," she replied.

"That'd put us near the Wicker Dam?"

"Yeah, I suppose." She stood and motioned at the surrounding landscape. "But this place, this town and the lake and everything, it wasn't on the map. We should have come across the Wicker by now, but instead we're miles off-track. Who knows where the dam is."

She slumped dejectedly back down on the bricks beside him. He felt the warmth of her body as she shivered against him and realised that they needed to get out of the cold. The wind had begun to pick up and dark clouds were moving over the face of the sun. Their clothes, or what was left of them, were now no more than wet rags. He hadn't had any outdoor experience, but he knew what resulted from the lethal combination of wet clothes and cold wind: hypothermia.

Josh helped Greer to her feet and they struggled through the remains of the ruined town. In places it was knee-deep in foul-smelling mud and clinging slime. Finally, exhausted and cold, they found shelter in a squat brick building that had managed to retain three of its four walls. Most of the roof lay scattered over the floor, yet one corner offered them some protection from the wind.

For a long time they sat huddled together, their

knees pressed up to their chins. Josh snatched glances
at Greer from the corner of his eye. She seemed to
be staring at some distant scene, lost in thought.
Even covered in mud, scratched and bruised from
their hike, wet hair plastered over her face, she still
looked beautiful, he thought. Suddenly, she sat up,
jolting Josh from his private reverie.

"What's up?" he asked. "You hear something?"

"No, I haven't heard a thing . . . but I've *seen*
something!" Greer said, rubbing her fingers over
the wall excitedly.

"Have you noticed how everything around here,
everything, is covered in this slime? It's like the stuff
that grows in my kid brother's aquarium."

Josh wondered where she was going with this.

"Sure. We were hiking in solid rain for more than
three days before Mt Darius erupted. The whole of
the Bellevue was soaking wet, remember?"

She ignored him. "Look at the floor," she
demanded.

"Just mud."

"Exactly! Mud! The ground's covered in mud
and the whole place is covered in slime!"

He looked at her uneasily, as if she'd become
slightly unhinged.

"Sure. Mud and slime . . . the island's thick

with it. So what?"

"Did you notice, Josh, that this whole island is covered in trees?"

Now she was really freaking him out.

"Of course. Once again, so what?"

Her eyes were blazing now. "The trees had no foliage! Not a single green leaf. Nothing! Just dead stumps. Did you see, Josh?"

He put a hand on her arm as if to calm her down. "Greer, the whole of Bellevue is dead tree stumps. The eruption and fire wiped out them all out! We've been walking through smouldering trees and stuff like this for days now."

She pulled her arm free of his hand. "No! This island's different! That's what I'm trying to say." She grabbed his hand and dragged him back outdoors.

The mist had lifted somewhat, blown away by the wind like a tattered spider's web.

"See!" she cried triumphantly, pointing to the trees that hemmed the dead town on all sides.

He looked. "Just more dead trees."

"Just more dead, *wet* trees! You said it yourself, Josh. Everything around here is wet! For the last two days, all we've seen has been ash-dry, scorched by the eruption. But everything in this valley, on this island, is soaking wet . . . no ash, no fire."

She was right. Josh took a closer look at the surrounding landscape, as if for the first time.

The island, and for that matter the steep hillsides on the other side of the lake, were sodden – not just drenched from heavy rain, but black and waterlogged, as if they had been totally submerged for a long time.

A century or more.

Greer was pointing to the surrounding hills. Running just below the ridge line, all the way around the valley, was a distinct line. "Check out those markings!"

"Looks like the watermark around the rim of a bath."

"Yeah. Everything above the rim is covered in ash, then suddenly everything below that mark looks as if it's been under water – in a bath like you said – including this town."

"The town? You reckon the town was, like, under water or something?"

"Flooded, I guess."

"And the whole island and the lake, right up to the top of those hills?"

"Must've been."

"That's a lot of water. Where'd all that water come from? Not a couple of days of heavy rain . . ."

"A hundred years of rain wouldn't fill this valley," she said.

"So where, how?"

She suddenly smiled – the kind of smile he'd seen her use in class so many times. The smile that told everybody, "I've got it figured!"

"I'd say it was deliberately done," she said. "Flooded on purpose."

Before Josh could respond, she was off down the remains of the muddy street, her head turning back and forth, searching for something.

"What are you looking for?" he called after her.

She had stopped and was pointing in triumph.

Josh scrambled and slipped through the mud to where she stood. She was pointing at the remnants of a large stone building. It looked as if it had once been elegant; the remains of two stone columns could still be seen. All but the façade had been reduced to waterlogged rubble and the stonework bore a green slime stain like everything else. Gaping holes where the windows had once been seemed to glare back at them like the empty eye sockets of a blackened skull.

Josh was looking for some clue. "What am I supposed to be looking at?"

"It's an old bank!" she cried, the joy of discovery

dancing in her eyes.

"So?"

"So, look above where the door used to be. What do you see?"

He peered at the damaged façade. It was aged and slime-covered, but, as the weak sunlight shifted, he was able to make out letters carved deep in the stonework. He spelled them aloud, as a young child would read a first book. "B A N K. Yeah, you were right, it's a bank. I still don't get why you're so excited."

"Can you make out the words before BANK?"

He moved closer, staring intently, annoyed that she seemed to be playing games with him.

"I can see a B and an L and an A, C, K. BLACK." He carried on. "The rest is pretty messed up, letters seem to be missing . . . R, I, V, E. . .that's all I get. BLACK RIVE."

"Black River! It's the Black River Bank!" she shouted exultantly.

Josh rubbed his forehead. "So, the town was called Black River? And it had a bank. What's so special about that? What's the big deal?"

Her green eyes flashed at him and he immediately kicked himself for sounding like a know-it-all.

"It *is* a 'big deal', as it happens," she said, her smile

returning as quickly as a spring shower, "because it explains why we couldn't find it on the map."

"Why?"

"The town of Black River disappeared over a hundred years ago!"

"What do you mean, disappeared?"

"Flooded . . . wiped off the map."

"Who flooded it?"

She stood, hands on hips, surveying the remains of Black River. "The guy who built the dam."

Josh looked up, startled. "The Wicker Dam?"

"Samuel Z Wicker III himself! He's the guy who flooded Black River to make a giant hydro lake to store water for generating power. I remember reading about it. He turned this whole valley into Lake Wicker."

"Then Lake Wicker must be nearby."

Greer looked at him in a strange kind of way.

"This *is* Lake Wicker, Josh, or what's left of it . . . the eruption must have damaged the Wicker Dam."

He looked around at the sheer height of the surrounding hills. "When the plug got pulled, the bath must've emptied big time!"

Greer nodded, her eyes widening as she looked around.

"And Black River rose up from the dead!"

Chapter Four

Early in the morning of the 12th of April, 1900, the town of Black River had indeed died. Drowned slowly and deliberately, as if some giant hand had forced its head under a billion gallons of water.

The drowning of the town was watched dispassionately by the very man who had ordered it, Samuel Z Wicker III. He stood atop the concrete structure that bore his name – the Wicker Dam.

He looked a little like a biblical prophet, legs apart, hands clutching the dam railing, snow-white hair blowing about his face. He was attired in a white suit of impeccable tailoring, a blood red tie precisely knotted at his throat and a matching kerchief geometrically positioned in his jacket pocket.

Everything about him spoke of an almost maniacal attention to detail. His luxuriant white moustache was clinically manicured, with not a single hair out of place. Even his white eyebrows, jutting out spectacularly from his large forehead, were trimmed to show-dog perfection. Only his eyes – grey with flecks of gold – hinted at an unpredictable savagery, barely contained.

Samuel Z Wicker had another quality that emanated from every pore of his immaculately groomed person. He was rich – obscenely, filthily rich. In his fine suit, reeking of wealth, he watched the thundering waters surge through the massive floodgates and drown the forested valley, choking the life from the little town of Black River.

Without moving his eyes from the scene below, he snatched at a fat blowfly that had impudently landed on his bull-like neck and squished the life from it, black juice trickling out between his fingers.

He remained unmoving all day, as if cast from white granite, until the last building sank from view and the town of Black River was no more. Then, with the sun setting in the distance over Mt Darius, he finally turned and snapped his fingers.

A rake-thin manservant sprang like a leopard from the shadows with a silver tray and cut crystal decanter and glass. He had been patiently standing in readiness all day for such a moment. In the employ of Samuel Z Wicker III, or the Great Man, as his employees referred to him, it certainly paid to anticipate the master's every whim. Failure to do so often ended painfully and sometimes even tragically.

While his servant poured brandy, the Great Man spoke for the first time that day. His voice was as precise as his attire, as his life, as his calculations. It was a voice that always boomed, a voice that commanded attention.

"The Portuguese called that lake Lago da Morte. Did you know that, Manolo?"

The manservant bowed obsequiously, averting his black eyes. "No, señor, I did not know. I knew it only as Black River Lake." He handed Samuel Z the crystal tumbler on the silver tray and stepped back into the shadows.

"Lago da Morte!" the Great Man continued, as if the manservant hadn't spoken at all. "Translated it means Lake of the Dead!" He gulped the brandy in one slug, then hurled the crystal tumbler over the edge of the dam and watched it spin into oblivion far below.

"Well, that stinking little town is at the bottom of

the Lake of the Dead now and can stay that way till Christ himself returns!"

His wild eyes burned molten, before flickering back to a cold slate grey. Then, with a malevolent smile, he addressed the startled Manolo. "I've decided to rename the new lake, Manolo. Can't have it known as Lake of the Dead. How do you like the sound of Lake Wicker, boy? Rolls off the tongue, don't you think?"

Manolo merely bowed low again as the Great Man swept past him, down the mighty causeway of his mighty dam.

The drowning of Black River and the creation of Lake Wicker had required a staggering amount of cold hard cunning and cold hard cash. And Samuel Z Wicker III apparently had a bottomless pit of both.

"The Millionaire Magnate" the press had named him, and he liked the ring of it, almost as much as he liked the ring of money pouring into his coffers. His father, Samuel Zeus Wicker II, a mildly successful haberdashery proprietor, had bequeathed him a meagre inheritance on his deathbed. Other men would have squandered the small sum on the gambling tables, on fine wine or whisky, or lost it all on some shady investment. Not the young Samuel Z. He had taken his puny inheritance and ruthlessly transformed it into a fortune of almost incalculable proportions.

The bulk of his vast wealth had come from the goldfields at St Lima. Not that the Great Man had ever rolled up his sleeves and dug a single shovelful of the notoriously hard red dirt himself. Oh, no.

He was, as ever, cunning as a desert rattler and shrewd enough to realise that the real fortune was to be made once the gold had been prised from the ground. For Samuel Z knew he could bet on other men's greed. So he built rough and ready frontier towns on the outskirts of the goldfields. They were towns designed for one thing and one thing only: to relieve the newly rich, but eternally stupid, prospectors of their golden nuggets. Banks, barbers and bars sprang up overnight, all owned to the last nail by Samuel Z Wicker III. Like a giant spider, he lured dusty goldminers to his sticky web; in their thousands they swarmed, and in their thousands they lost every last cent, leaving them empty husks to be blown away by the wind.

Samuel Z could not have cared less. Sitting in the

centre of his web, he was attuned to every vibration in his labyrinth of enterprises, ready to strike with deadly force if anything or anyone disrupted his web of greed.

When eventually the goldfields dried up and the prospectors had been stripped of everything it was possible to take, Samuel Z cast his steely eyes further afield, all the way to the Bellevue Wilderness.

The Bellevue was named for an eighteenth-century explorer, Captain Ezra Bellevue, who had perished mysteriously while charting its vast wilderness. Dominated by a dormant volcano named Mt Darius, the Bellevue stretched over more than a hundred thousand hectares of pristine forestland, lakes and mountains.

And it was almost entirely uninhabited.

This was perfect for the Great Man's purposes. For more than fifty years he had dreamed of constructing a city – not like the frontier towns of St Lima, but an enormous mega-city. It would be a city to rival New York and London. A conurbation of international fame. A metropolis that would be owned and controlled to the very last brick by Samuel Z Wicker III!

From the moment he first glimpsed the vast wilderness of the Bellevue, he knew he had found the perfect setting for his soaring dream city – a city he had already named Metropolene.

Although the huge tract of land was largely uninhabited, it was owned by the Great Western Timber Company, which was run by a hard-drinking, hard-dealing bulldog of a man: Butch Tibbins.

When the Great Man's agents first approached Butch with an offer to purchase his hundred thousand hectares of prime forestland, they had been sent packing, first with drunken threats, then with fiery buckshot! Butch Tibbins had been famously quoted as yelling after them, "You tell that old cockroach Wicker that he can have Bellevue – over my dead body!"

Samuel Z had simply smiled his death-mask smile and retreated to the centre of his web to bide his time. He ordered Metropolene's planners to carry right on as if the deed to Bellevue was already in his tailored pocket.

A series of events, still shrouded in mystery, handed the Great Man that deed on a silver platter. First, the Great Western Timber Company's main mill was destroyed in a devastating fire that quickly spread to consume thousands of hectares of pristine forest. A drunken Butch Tibbins was found near the blaze asleep, the remains of a smouldering cigar still gripped in his stubby fingers.

Tibbins was speedily convicted of the arson that had destroyed the forest and bankrupted his company. He swore black and blue all through the trial that the whisky he drank that fateful night had been drugged and that, in a comatose state, he'd been dumped at the scene of the blaze, cigar in hand.

The jury didn't believe a word of it. (Nor could they. Samuel Z Wicker had bought and paid for every one of their verdicts.) Butch Tibbins was sentenced to thirty years behind bars and was dragged away, cursing Samuel Z with every breath. "I'll get you, Wicker! I'll make you pay for this with every last pint of your filthy blood!"

The second unexplained mystery was how Butch Tibbins was able to escape the iron bars of his prison cell and get his hands on a double-barrelled shotgun. It was as if the guards had simply left the keys and the gun outside his cell door and disappeared for the night.

Without dispute is the fact that, shotgun in hand, Tibbins stormed into the offices of the Samuel Z Wicker consortium, breathing fire and ranting like a madman.

When the sheriff and his men finally arrived,

they found Butch sprawled over a huge map of Metropolene on Samuel Z's desk, stone dead, a shotgun in his cold hands.

The Great Man claimed self-defence – that Tibbins had burst into his office in a drunken rage threatening to kill him. So he'd fired a single revolver shot to Butch's forehead and called the authorities.

The law agreed wholeheartedly – definitely self-defence – and Tibbins's body was dragged away. No one cared to comment on the six bullet holes in his back!

Thus Samuel Z Wicker bought, for a laughable sum, the deed to the entire Bellevue Forest; one hundred thousand hectares, and all, prophetically, acquired over Butch Tibbins's dead body.

Even the devastating forest fire proved to be beneficial, for it saved the Great Man from having to pay a single cent to clear the land for his dream city. It was almost as if the whole thing was planned.

Construction was about to begin in earnest. Yet, before one paving stone could be laid for Metropolene, there was still one giant obstacle to overcome – power.

A city the size of Metropolene would need a staggering source of power to run it. And, because the Bellevue Forest was a wilderness, there was no ready-to-use power supply for more than 1000 kilometres in any direction. A power source would need to be built from scratch.

And so, one brilliantly sunny spring morning, the Great Man himself stood on the recently cleared forest site and unrolled a massive blueprint for the assembled press reporters to see.

"A city of the grandeur I propose will need power – and plenty of it!" he boomed from a raised wooden platform. "Therefore I will build the largest dam ever seen. Enough to power my Metropolene forever!"

He paused for a wry smile. "I have humbly chosen to name it . . . the Wicker Dam!"

There was enthusiastic clapping and a general buzz of awed excitement until a reporter interrupted the applause to question the Great Man. "Won't your dam . . . your Wicker Dam, sir . . . require a hydro lake of huge proportions to generate the power you'll need?"

Samuel Z eyed him from his platform like a snake about to strike. "I have already planned for such a lake. I intend to flood the Black River Valley, creating a colossal hydro lake to generate the power for my Metropolene."

More thunderous clapping.

The reporter, however, continued his impudent line of questioning. "Excuse me, sir! But wouldn't that mean flooding huge stretches of forest, as well as the town of Black River itself?"

The assembled press and dignitaries turned to stare at the obdurate reporter. No one in the assembled group had ever heard of the town of Black River before. Hardly anyone in the outside world had, either. It was an isolated, backwater town strung out along one muddy street on a small island in the middle of an insignificant lake into which the Black River flowed.

The population was small – only a hundred or so folk, mostly timber workers, hunters and drifters. It boasted few substantial buildings: a general store, a saloon or two, and the Black River Bank. The rest was a jumble of old timber and brick dwellings, all in sad decline. The only way in or out was by boat or barge. But few folk ever ventured over the dark lake waters to Black River, unless for a very good reason.

The truth was, there was never a good reason to visit Black River. Surrounded by steep hills, it spent much of the year hunched in gloomy shadow, the sun barely reaching the rooftops. That's what gave the lake its inky blackness.

It was the early Portuguese explorers who had

first stumbled on the black waters of the lake. They had cursed it with the name Lago da Morte, though no one was sure why. According to the few accounts that remained, they had encountered something sinister in the primeval waters surrounding the island and town. Something they referred to as "espirito mau" – an evil spirit.

Whatever the truth of the matter, bad luck had attached itself to the town of Black River ever since. Few even knew of its existence, let alone cared for its fate.

Except Samuel Z Wicker III.

He knew every detail of that forgotten backwater, as a man might meticulously inspect an unusual beetle before spearing it with a pin and watching it slowly die.

His calculations were, as usual, precise and clinical. He needed a mighty lake to power his mighty hydro station – and to create a mighty lake he would need to flood a mighty valley. If a pesky, snot stain of a town happened to be in that valley, well, too bad! He would simply drown it out of existence.

The simple folk of Black River would see the light and move away, given enough financial incentive. For those who stubbornly refused – well, maybe they would need something more persuasive . . .

So, on that brilliant spring morning, with the assembled reporters waiting for the Great Man's answer, Samuel Z Wicker III dismissively waved his manicured hand and boomed, "There'll be no one left in the town of Black River, gentlemen. It will become a ghost town. When a billion gallons of water begin to fill that valley, no one will shed a solitary tear for that god-forsaken town, I can assure you. No one!"

Chapter Five

Josh and Greer stood in the mud where the main street would have run and stared at the sad remains. They tried to imagine a thriving town, with people in the streets, horses and carts rumbling by, shops filled with goods, but it had all been washed away, leaving only the ghosts of the past.

"We must be the first people to see Black River for more than a hundred years," Josh said at last. "Wonder where they all went when they left?"

"Bet they'd have secrets worth telling if they could speak from their graves," murmured Greer, still lost in thought.

Josh felt a cold hand run up his spine and, when he shivered, it was not due to the chill wind.

"I'm betting one of those secrets was that thing we saw in the lake."

Greer's face drained of colour. "That's assuming there's just the one, Josh."

For a moment they looked at each other, then both turned to scan the lake. As the afternoon light faded, the cold shadows on the water were lengthening.

"I'm thinking we should stay here on this island, at least for tonight," Josh said, shivering.

"But what about trying to get to the Wicker?" Greer asked.

"I think, if the dam's burst like you said, there won't be much left up there anyway. Our best chance could be staying put on this island until someone finds us."

Greer scrunched up her forehead in thought. "Kind of makes sense. But, if they don't come looking by the end of tomorrow, then we've got no other choice . . ."

"What do you mean?" Josh asked, though he already knew the answer.

Greer's eyes were wide with fear now. "We'll have to swim back over the lake together or we'll end up dead like everything else in Black River."

Josh didn't want to say that, if they got back in

the water, they'd probably end up dead anyway. And now she'd added to his fears by raising the possibility that there might be more than one creature out there in the black water! Yet, the more he thought about it, the more he had to agree with her.

Back home, his cousins had a farm with a huge pond at its centre. Nothing fancy, just a dirty, kidney-shaped water hole. They had swum in it most summers until it was overtaken by black eels. They seemed to thrive, to multiply in the swampy water. Josh had looked on in morbid fascination as his cousins had thrown fish guts into the pond and watched the swirling mass of slithery black eels fight for the food.

They had made spears of broom handles with rusty nails lashed to the ends, and with these crude weapons they had stabbed the dirty water for eels. Josh had actually managed to spear one. Its writhing body, still pierced through the middle by his spear, flopped about on the dry grass. He hadn't known how to put it out of its misery. He'd tried to whack it against a tree and knock its head with a large rock but the eel still writhed and squirmed. So he'd simply plucked the spear out and watched it slither back into the pond, bleeding profusely. The other eels had pounced on it and hungrily devoured it, tearing it to pieces in seconds.

With the evening creeping in and the cold wind sapping what little body heat they had, they returned to take shelter in the remains of the Black River Bank. The interior was dark and dank, draped with slime. However, the remains of a long wooden counter still ran down one wall with some cupboard doors and drawers still roughly intact. Josh tried to force them open, in the vain hope that they might contain something edible – canned food or maybe even a candle . . . But they were all rotten to his touch; rotten and empty, some full of pulped paper, green with slime.

While Greer watched, he continued his fruitless searching.

"You won't find anything in this mess. It's been a hundred years since anyone's been near this place. Anyway it was a bank, not a grocery," she said.

He didn't answer, though he knew she was right. She always seemed to be right. Yet, driven by a need to do something, anything, he continued poking around. That's when he noticed the door.

At the rear of the bank, almost totally covered in fallen debris from the collapse of the roof above, stood a door. He quickly clambered over the rubble to take a closer look.

Every other door in this ruined town was rotting away or completely missing, the sparse remains of their wooden frames hanging from rusted hinges. Yet this door was remarkably intact, with patches of dark green paint still visible.

As Josh removed the chaos of rubble around it, he realised why it had survived a century of immersion. It was solid metal – rust-pitted and badly scarred, but still as solid as the day it was installed.

He called to Greer, who reluctantly left her sheltered spot to join him. Together they cleared away the remaining debris until the whole door was visible.

At its centre was a large brass handle, green and corroded with age. Josh exerted all his strength to turn it but it refused to budge.

That was when Greer noticed the brass keyhole beneath it. "It's been locked," she said. "Locked for a hundred years."

Josh kicked the metal door in frustration. He had hoped that whatever was on the other side had somehow been sealed from the black lake water. Determined not to give up, he motioned to Greer to help him pick up a solid beam lying on the floor.

"What are you going to do with that?"

"Barge the door . . . break it down if I have to."

"But why? I've told you already, there will be nothing of any value left in this place. It's a ghost town."

He picked up one end of the beam. "Are you going to help me or what?"

When she still hesitated, he added, "It's not like we've got much else to do."

Reluctantly, she grabbed the other end.

The first blow shook them more than the door.

"Satisfied?" asked Greer.

"Just a couple more . . . it's weakening," he lied.

On the third blow, more to his surprise than hers, the door moved slightly.

He inspected the damage. The actual door was still as solid as when they had found it, the handle and lock stubbornly rigid. Yet the battering had loosened the bricks and mortar surrounding it. Cracks had appeared.

With new strength and enthusiasm, they banged away for another twenty minutes. Suddenly, the door fell inwards in a shower of bricks and dust.

For a minute or two, they stood speechless, staring into the dark void beyond the smashed doorway. Then Greer picked up a brick and ran her fingers over it. "It's dry! Bone dry!" she said incredulously. "Whatever was sealed behind that door has remained waterproof for one hundred years . . . at the bottom of the lake!"

Josh was already stepping over the rubble and into the dark space beyond. "Let's see what the good folk of Black River left locked up all this time!"

The answer was not long in coming. With a howl so loud it echoed through the ruined town, Josh sprang back from the gaping doorway.

Greer grabbed his arm in alarm as Josh gasped for breath, his face drained of blood.

"You scared the living daylights out of me, Josh, yelling like that! What are you trying to do . . . raise the dead?"

He pointed through the doorway, his hand visibly shaking. "Don't think the dead will be rising any time soon!"

She stepped past him into the dusky room. As her eyes adjusted, she saw what Josh had seen. Her reaction was similar, but louder.

Lying on the dusty floor, face upwards and arms outstretched, as if imploring them for help, its skin the colour of old leather, was the perfectly preserved body of an old man.

He was wearing scruffy clothes: a pair of torn, faded trousers, a dirty grey flannel shirt unbuttoned to reveal a stained singlet. His hair was steel grey, wiry and unkempt, his chin bristling with stubble, eyes locked open in death.

In his right hand, clutched in century-old rigor mortis, was a sheaf of yellowed papers that declared, in spidery but precise longhand, that this was "The Last Testament of Gerard Tarras".

Yet it was not only the discovery of his body that stunned Greer and Josh – it was the nature of his death that shocked them most. When the horror of their discovery had worn off, they drew gingerly closer and carefully took the papers from the old man's hand. Scrawled on the top page, below his name, were the chilling words:

I hear the floods above me . . . breathing comes harder and I know that this vault will be my tomb . . . I have no kith or kin, nobody to mourn me . . . Still I pray that God will avenge my death at the hand of Samuel Z Wicker! I will, at least, die in the knowledge that my life's quest was not in vain. IT LIVES!

Gerard Tarras

Chapter Six

Gerard Tarras lived with a dead body in his cabin.

The cabin was high in the hills surrounding Black River and its dark lake. Winter and summer, smoke bled from the chimney and mist stalked the forest that pressed in from every side. No one made the journey up the steep, rocky trail to his isolated cabin, and that was the way he liked it.

Gerard Tarras was a hermit, with no need for human companionship. For seventy years he'd lived this way and for at least fifty of those years, he had shared his cabin with a dead man.

What was left of the body – bleached bones and skull – was laid out on a table. He had painstakingly assembled most of the fragments; only some finger joints and a rib or two were missing.

There were still threads of a jacket clinging stubbornly to the shoulder blade and, on the left foot, a piece of decayed leather was all that remained of a boot.

Gerard liked to hold the skull in his hands, cupped like a bowl of soup. The empty eye sockets stared out at him, the yellowed teeth forming a garish smile. And Gerard Tarras would smile back in his own cracked-tooth way.

Once or twice a year, he would travel down the steep mountain trail and cross the lake to Black River for supplies. Then he would scurry back up the trail to resume his life in splendid isolation, alone with only the skeleton on his table for company.

The townsfolk paid him no heed. Black River was full of such characters: old prospectors, army deserters and drifters. Gerard, in his grubby coat, dishevelled grey hair poking out from under his battered hat, was just another piece of human flotsam that had washed down the river.

Only a few folk knew his full name; the fat proprietor of the dingy general store was one. "Ah! If it ain't old Gerard Tarras! Thought you must be dead and smelling up there in that hovel you call a cabin."

Gerard would spit a stream of filthy black tobacco juice on the floorboards at his feet. "The only thing smelling to high heaven is the prices you charge in this stink-hole you call a store, Bert McGaffey!"

"Well, old man, take your business elsewhere if you please!"

There was no other store in Black River. So Gerard would fill his pack with supplies, muttering through his whiskers about the exorbitant cost.

"You still got that skeleton living with you up in the hills, old man?" Bert McGaffey would ask tauntingly.

"Aye! And it be better company than you, or the whole town of Black River, for that matter."

"So, you still think there's something to that half-baked fairytale then."

Gerard's eyes would smoulder. "Ain't no fairytale. His journal proves it!"

"Scribblings of a fool! You should bury his bones and his crazy story!"

Gerard had heard it all before. He knew it was pointless to argue with Bert McGaffey, so he simply paid for his supplies, spat one last time on the store floor, and banged the door shut after him.

Back in the cabin, with the first blast of winter howling through the cracks in the log walls, he would light the fire with frozen fingers, then shuffle over to the slab of pine that served as his dining table and workbench. The skeleton lay amid the detritus of many years: chipped mugs, boxes of cartridges, melted candles and a stunning assortment of dead insects clustered around the spluttering kerosene lamp.

"Seventy years," he mused, as he held the skull up to the lamplight. "Soon I'll be like you, my friend. And your secret will, most likely, die right along with me."

He placed the skull gently back on the table as if he were laying the head of a loved one back on a pillow.

"Fat Bert McGaffey asked after you. Usual stuff. Said your story was 'the scribblings of a crazy fool.'" He looked deep into the skull's empty eyes. "Were you crazy, my friend? Or am I the crazy one for believing you all these long years?"

He pulled up a chair to the blazing fire. Outside, the wind moaned. He stared into the flames for a long time, thinking back to the fateful day he'd stumbled on the remains of the man who now lay on his kitchen table.

It had been fifty years ago. Gerard had returned to his family's cabin at Black River after hunting deep in the Bellevue, up near the foothills of Mt Darius. He had returned after a month away, only to find that his pa had died the week before.

"Consumption," the doctor had said. "Coughed up his stomach in bloody pieces."

Gerard was the only child; his ma had passed away at his birth.

The doc had urged him to deal with the body quickly. Black River had no formal cemetery, so Gerard had taken the body of his father, wrapped in a burlap sack, and looked for a place to bury him.

On the northern tip of the island, some distance from Black River, was a steep, forested hill rising from a remote and rocky bay where few people ever ventured.

It was here, on the edge of the tree line above the shore, that he had begun to dig a grave. He dug deep to keep wild animals from getting to his pa's body.

Knee-deep in the black soil of the grave, his spade struck something hard. He had bent down to take a look, expecting it to be no more than a rock. To his amazement, he discovered something else. This spot had been the final resting place of another person.

Gerard had carefully exhumed the bones. They were the remains of a man, the flesh decayed long ago. And lying beside the body was another remarkable discovery – a leather-bound journal, wrapped in the remnants of a canvas pouch. The pages were brittle and in places completely decayed but enough remained for Gerard to glean the story of the man who had written on them, the man whose bones now lay at his feet.

First, however, he had buried his father and marked his grave with a cairn of rocks. Then he had collected all the bones, placed them in his burlap sack and taken them back home.

Over the ensuing weeks, alone in the cabin, he had meticulously separated each brittle page of the dead man's journal and pieced together what he could of his writings. Then, by flickering candle light, he had read and reread the sad saga they detailed.

It was the journal of Captain Ezra Bellevue, who was thought to have been lost in the vast untamed wilderness in 1795, while on an exploratory foray. Neither his body, nor those of his companions, had ever been found. The wilderness had subsequently been named in his memory.

Gerard now read the truth of his final days:

As I write this final account, I fully realise that the

events I must record are so unbelievable as to be dismissed by whoever reads them as the ravings of a madman. But I swear on all that is holy that what I write is true.

I am the only one of my travelling companions left alive and indeed my own life fades fast, due to my wounds and the gangrene that has now infected them.

Of such a terrible fate we had no idea when we five bold adventurers departed Fort Hanning early in April 1795 . . .

Now, gripped with a gangrenous fever, weak and at times delirious, I pen these words. Despite my pain, I know with startling clarity that I am dying and will never leave this island alive.

I therefore write these last words as testimony to my brave companions and also as a warning to whomever finds this journal.

PRAY BEWARE OF THE BLACK WATERS AND OF THE EVIL THAT RESIDES IN THIS LAKE OF THE DEAD!

Captain Ezra Bellevue, 1795

Gerard had mulled over those words well into the early hours of each morning, the fire dead and cold at his feet.

Captain Bellevue's description of the creature that had taken his companions' lives swirled through his mind . . .

It had a serpentine body, black as sin itself, sleek and oily, pockmarked and pitted with scars. In size, I guessed it to be as long as a well-grown tree and as round at the girth as well. It bore some resemblance to a snake, with black eyes devoid of life, yet its massive mouth was toothed like that of a deep-sea fish. It looked, to my petrified eyes, like nothing less than some giant eel of a prehistoric origin.

Could it be possible that the very lake that surrounded Black River contained a prehistoric creature of gargantuan proportions? A man-eater?

Gerard had spent twenty years on the lake's edge and never caught sight of such a thing. Had it died? Or was it never there at all? Could he find it?

So began a passion, some would say an obsession, to find proof of the existence of the creature that the dying captain had so tragically described.

As he had always been content to keep to his own company, Gerard Tarras felt no need to share his grisly discovery with anyone else. Not until he had the proof. And so the captain's skeleton, painstakingly reassembled, and his leather journal, remained hidden from view in Gerard's cabin.

He spent long months searching the northern end of the island, camping out in all weathers, retracing the captain's last days. Yet he found nothing, except for the skeletal remains of an old canoe.

He returned to his cabin only when the snows of winter made exploration impossible. His pa had left him the small amount of money he had saved in a life of hard struggle. Like thousands of others, his pa had laboured in the goldfields of St Lima and had extracted, after much blood and tears, a mere fistful of nuggets. Not nearly enough to call himself rich, but enough to pass on to Gerard in his will.

As Gerard's passion overtook him, this small inheritance became his only support. But his needs were basic: flour and meat, a pouch of tobacco, whisky now and then and books. He had sent away to the big cities in the north for books on palaeontology, the fledgling science of prehistoric fossils. Soon these tomes lined the walls of his small cabin.

He had had no formal education; in fact, he had barely been able to read until the age of ten. But, such was his desire to learn all he could about the mysterious creature in the journal, he had thrown himself into mastering the written word with a vengeance.

His few acquaintances soon gave up on him

entirely: "Spends all his days cooped up in his cabin with them books!"

To escape their prying eyes and wagging tongues, he retreated up into the Bellevue hills and built himself another cabin. There he would pore over his books, reading voraciously of fossilised discoveries in Great Britain, North America and Asia. He was determined to understand what kind of creature Captain Ezra Bellevue had encountered.

At first his readings led him to believe it must be *Deinosuchus*, an ancestor of the crocodile from the Cretaceous period, which grew to a staggering fifteen metres in length. Yet *Deinosuchus*, or for that matter its Jurassic crocodilian cousin *Steneosaurus*, with its elongated nose, had legs and razor-sharp claws. Captain Bellevue's description of the creature was that of a legless serpent, devoid of appendages. The journal described no such arms or legs.

There were discoveries of sea creatures named plesiosaurs. They roamed the great southern seas, more than twelve metres in length, with enormous wing-like fins. Although they had many of the characteristics of the beast in Captain Bellevue's journal, Gerard had ruled them out as well.

"Nothing less than some giant eel of a prehistoric origin." That's what the terrified men had seen.

A giant eel. Gerard searched his books for descriptions of eels long enough in length to match that of the journal. The serpent eel, *Ophisurus serpens*, found in the eastern Atlantic and off the islands of New Zealand, seemed probable. They had long, conical bodies, narrow anal and dorsal fins, a large mouth with a single row of razor-sharp teeth in each jaw and an even larger row of teeth on the roof of their mouths. Sailors and fishermen had often mistaken these black creatures for sea snakes – hence the name "serpent eel". Yet they seldom grew longer than one to one and a half metres.

He turned next to books that recounted fabled sightings of fabulously horrible sea monsters, hoping to link their lurid descriptions with that of anything in the fossil record. The tales he read by firelight in his wintry cabin were nothing short of terrifying. It seemed that Captain Ezra Bellevue and his brave crew were not the only ones to have encountered such fearsome creatures.

Gerard read with horrified fascination an account from the early 1800s, not so long before his own birth, by a fisherman named Jacobi Cubbins. With his brother, Cubbins had sighted a "long serpent of hideous length and undulating terror" while out at sea. This creature they estimated at more than thirty metres long, with a head of frightening proportions, two metres from jaw to neck. The huge sea creature then began to pursue the horrified brothers.

"It moved upon us with astonishing speed, its foul tail snake-like in movement, in sideways curves and contortions, like that of an eel."

As it passed astern of their boat, they saw its glistening teeth and its "evil-looking eyes, black as death".

It was only a fast-moving fog bank that saved them and they escaped to shore with their lives and their alarming tale.

Other sailors reported similar sightings, some of them even more horrific. In 1798, the crew of HMS *Glorious*, while drifting in the Coral Sea after a tropical storm had disabled their main mast, came upon a terrifying creature.

We saw the Sea Beast rise up out the sea; spines ran down its ghastly back and its mouth gaped open, revealing rows of teeth so sharp and deadly as to sever a man's body with a single bite! It reared back as a cobra might afore striking, and then attacked our small ship, tearing off the whole port bow in a single strike! Sixteen of our crew were plunged into the water and we still on-board could only watch

in horror as the beast tore them to bloody shreds.
As it loomed to attack us a second time, we let
loose with a volley from our cannon and drove the
Sea Beast to its deep abode, thus saving our souls!

Gerard read and reread these fabulous tales of amazing encounters. He was not sure which parts were fact and which were fiction. Many experts believed the "giant sea serpent" to be nothing more than a large oarfish – a giant herring with pelvic fins and an elongated body, which could reach up to six metres in length. Oarfish had the habit of lingering near the surface when sick or dying, and often washed up on isolated shores. They had hideous heads, but were not known to be predators of man or ship at all.

Still, Gerard concluded, a common thread was emerging from all the accounts. The creature that each witness saw was malevolent in the extreme, with a taste for human flesh. And it was large – extremely large – and ancient.

Whatever it was that Captain Ezra Bellevue had seen first-hand in the lake was obviously a throwback to some prehistoric era. It had thrived in the dark, deep waters of this landlocked lake for a dozen millennia or more, defying all odds, breeding in its mutated way – an eel of giant proportions.

An eel that fed on the flesh of fish, animal . . . and human.

At the end of all his studies, he was convinced of two things. First, the giant eel was like nothing seen or recorded before. Second, that it was still alive and thriving in Black River Lake. And he, Gerard Tarras, was determined to find it.

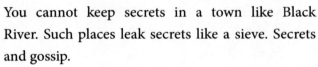

You cannot keep secrets in a town like Black River. Such places leak secrets like a sieve. Secrets and gossip.

So, the more Gerard Tarras tried to keep his secrets, the more gossip spread like smallpox, and with a similar result. Soon he couldn't walk through the muddy main street of Black River without being followed by whispers and avoided by all as a crazy man.

"Thinks there be somethin' in our lake!" the gossips sneered.

"Somethin' big and nasty, fit to tear a man to pieces!"

"I hear, from reliable sources, that the crazy old fool keeps a human skeleton on his kitchen table! Call me old-fashioned, but that just isn't proper; it's the type of thing a depraved person would do!"

"And see him always down by the lake edge. Practically lives there! Poking and digging for bones. What's he expect to find?"

"I hope that, if there is some big 'un in them waters, it jolly well rises up and swallows that old coot Tarras, and right soon! He brings bad luck to Black River, right and all!"

Such talk was always followed with much nodding of heads and furious puffing of pipes.

It wasn't just the men who spent time disparaging Gerard and his work. The women of Black River were equally adept at stabbing the knife of gossip into his back, and giving it a cruel turn as well.

"No wonder he ain't wed," they'd say, gathered along the counter of the general store like a flock of ravens. "What God-fearing woman would share home and hearth with a man that has human bones on the same table where he eats?"

"He's not right in the head! Gripped by finding a creature that God in his heaven never would have created. That be evil work."

So it was no surprise that Gerard avoided the town and the town avoided him. He would search the kilometres of lake edge only in inclement weather when he was sure to be alone and to be left alone as well.

When not scouring the lake shore, he retreated to his isolated cabin and only made the journey to Black River to get supplies and pay a visit to Fulford Dickers, the manager of the Black River Bank.

Pompous and frayed, with a face like a melted candle and the eyes of a rat, Fulford Dickers would lead him to the green metal door of the bank's one vault and, with an unnecessary flourish, open it with a large brass key. The vault was practically bare. Black River, after all, was far from being a prosperous town. Yet inside was Gerard's inheritance, locked away in an old, gunmetal grey ammunition box, along with the few other valuable possessions he kept there for safekeeping. With every passing year, the nuggets in that box became fewer and fewer.

He would take a piece of gold nugget and place it into Fulford Dickers's sweaty paw for assaying, avoiding the manager's rat eyes and their greedy gleam. That done, he would collect his payment in cold cash from the prissy clerk at the long wooden counter and depart as hurriedly as he could.

Back to the hills, back to the search . . .

Fifty years had slipped through his now gnarled fingers. And still no sign of the giant, eel-like creature that plagued his every waking moment, and his dreams as well.

He had uncovered bones though – tonnes of them. They littered his cabin in boxes, crates and sacks. Animal bones, bird bones, fish bones and even human bones. Some were fresh, some old, and many ancient.

There were fossils, too. Pressed in rock, their delicate swirls marked out spines and fins, finger bones splayed in death, their tissues long rotted away. The soft sediment surrounding the Black River had proved to be rich in fossil deposits. Yet, sadly, he found nothing remotely comparable to the size of the creature in Captain Bellevue's journal.

But, rather than dampening his spirits, this absence had served only to fuel his obsession. After all, he concluded, alone in his cabin surrounded by his grisly collection of bones, what else did he have to live for?

He was more than seventy now, with no family or friends left in the world. The folk of Black River had long turned their backs on the crazy hermit in the hills. Most of those who had known him in his younger days had died or merely drifted off, leaving the town to slip slowly into the sediment of yesteryear, much like Gerard's fossils. He was destined to die alone in his cramped cabin, unknown, unloved, the mystery of his giant eel unsolved.

However, two startling events changed everything. The first was a fire; the second was the construction of the Wicker Dam.

On the morning of his seventy-first birthday, Gerard was having his once-yearly shave, outdoors, using a bucket of cold water and a shard of mirror hung from a tree just above his ramshackle cabin.

He saw the two men before they saw him. They were approaching the cabin through the trees, not up the trail. Putting down his rusty razor, Gerard had thought about calling out to them, stopping them in their tracks. However, years spent hunting had taught him when to stay put. It had also taught him to smell trouble, much as a deer senses danger. And these men, crouched and approaching his cabin from the shadow of the forest, were most definitely trouble.

He watched them peering through his grimy windows, then moving in opposite directions around his cluttered porch. They spoke not a word, but motioned to each other with hand signals.

Gerard was of two minds whether to confront them openly, demanding to know what they wanted and telling them to get the heck off his property.

That's when he saw the guns.

Lake Of The Dead

The strangers were armed, each with a double-barrelled shotgun, and the bigger of the two had a revolver holstered at his hips.

Gerard cursed the fact that his own rifle was hanging inside his cabin above the fireplace. He reached down to pick up an old axe handle lying nearby, never once taking his eyes from the two strangers below.

They had disappeared on the far side of the cabin. Bent almost in half, Gerard ran around the side of the woodpile, keeping out of sight, his heart pounding.

He never had visitors, ever. Few folk even knew how to find the trail to his isolated home. These guys weren't paying Gerard a social visit, that was for sure. They meant business, but he couldn't think what the nature of that business might be.

Suddenly, he heard the shattering of glass, then the thud of something landing and rolling on the timber floorboards of his cabin. He dashed around to the front porch and straight into the path of one of the men, who froze, shotgun in hand, like a cornered bear.

Gerard raised his axe handle, expecting a blast of buckshot; he failed to see the other man move swiftly behind him from the shadows of the porch.

Next thing he knew, a rifle butt was crashing down on the back of his skull and he was falling over the side of the porch like a sack of cement.

Before blackness overtook him, he was aware of the smell of smoke, the sound of crackling flames, two shadowy figures disappearing into the forest, then nothing more.

Gerard awoke sometime in the night with a blazing headache, the back of his head matted and tacky with dried blood. Staggering to his feet, he was met with a horrific sight. His cabin was no more, just a pile of smoking rafters and smouldering embers. He made a desperate attempt to forage among the ruins to save what he could of his precious bone collection. But the white-hot heat of the embers drove him back.

By morning, when the embers had cooled and only wisps of smoke hung over the charred remains, he realised all was lost. Gerard Tarras sat down on his chopping block and wept.

For a whole day he sat there, staring at the destruction of a lifetime's work: the fossils and bones he had meticulously prised from the earth, the hundreds of books he had pored over by lamplight.

The remains of Captain Ezra Bellevue and his journal had turned to ash, blown away by the cold morning wind.

Who could be behind such wanton destruction? Why him? And why burn down his cabin?

The next morning, he left the burned remains of his home forever and headed resolutely down the mountain trail to Black River, bent on revenge.

The jetty was unusually deserted so he helped himself to the solitary rowboat and rowed across the dark lake to the town.

As he headed up the road from the lake to Black River, he was aware of something strange and sinister. At first he couldn't figure out what it was that made him so uneasy. Then it struck him. It was the silence.

There were no sounds, except for the birds and the soft lapping of the lake against the rocky shore. But no human noise at all.

The town was normally resonant with the clatter of horses, people shouting greetings, the bang of a hammer or slam of a door. This morning there was nothing.

The reason soon became apparent. As he walked the main street in a state of shock, he realised that Black River had become a ghost town. The windows of the shops were boarded up; the general store was dark and empty, with nothing on the shelves. There was no sign of Bert McGaffey and his mocking taunts. No horses tied to hitching rails, no wagons, no people bundled up against the chill.

His panic rose as he hurried to the Black River Bank. The door was ajar; he pushed it open and stepped inside. Papers littered the floor. The counter was bare and unattended. It seemed everyone had left in a hurry.

Then he heard a noise from the rear, the scraping of a box across the floor. There was someone in the vault. Gerard swung the heavy metal door wide and stepped inside. Fulford Dickers was stooped over a metal ammunition box, crowbar in hand. It was Gerard's safe deposit box.

The startled manager whirled around at the sound of the vault door swinging on its hinges, his rat eyes flickering.

"You!" he gasped, backing away. "I thought you were . . ."

"Dead?" snarled Gerard. "You thought I was dead and burnt to ash, didn't you?"

"No! I mean . . . I'd heard about the fire and I assumed . . ."

"Assumed what? That I wouldn't be needing my gold nuggets any longer?" Gerard snatched the crowbar from the bank manager's trembling hand.

Fulton Dickers dropped to his knees, his bottom lip trembling uncontrollably.

"I swear, Mr Tarras, I was only removing your gold for safekeeping!"

"Safekeeping or *your* keeping?" cried Gerard, raising the crowbar.

"No . . . safekeeping, I assure you! You must have seen the town . . . Everything's gone, closed; everyone's gone! I was merely taking your box to another location . . ."

"Why?" Gerard demanded. "What's happened to Black River. Has some sort of disease cleared the town?"

"It's no disease . . . it's the dam. The dam is coming!"

"Dam? What are you talking about, man?"

Fulford Dickers stared at the old man for a moment, stunned and perplexed. He was about to say, "Where have you been all this time?" but realised Gerard had been cut off from the sweeping events that had rocked Black River in the past twelve months.

He took a seat on an empty crate, mopping his brow, his eyes flicking nervously towards Gerard and the crowbar.

"Well, Mr Tarras, since you last came to town

there have been, er, significant changes to Black River. All on account of the new dam that Samuel Z Wicker III is building downstream . . ."

Gerard prodded him with the crowbar.

"Hold your horses, fella! Who did you say was building this dam?"

"Samuel Z Wicker III. He's a millionaire developer. Bought himself the whole of the Bellevue Forest from the bankrupt Great Western Timber Company and plans to build a brand new city in these parts. But he needs power first. That's why he's constructing a giant dam . . . He's going to flood this whole valley and Black River as well; turn it all into one enormous hydro lake!"

Gerard was stunned for a moment. He rubbed the back of his head with his free hand. It was still throbbing and sticky from the previous day's attack.

"You're telling me some rich buzzard flies into the Bellevue and wants to build a dam – a city – in the middle of nowhere! And wants to flood the valley to do it? And the whole town just ups and leaves?"

Fulford Dickers's shoulders slumped and he stared at his boots.

"Mr Wicker was extremely persuasive. He offered to purchase the whole town, with generous cash settlements."

"You mean the whole stinkin' town took bribes to leave! What about those who didn't want to go?"

There was a pause, then Fulford Dickers glanced anxiously up at Gerard.

"Let's just say that Mr Samuel Z Wicker is not the kind of man you can say no to. He has certain gentlemen with him who ensure that his wishes are complied with."

Gerard's eyes flamed. "You mean, he has thugs who'll deal to you if you don't do as he wants. Thugs who carry shotguns and burn down cabins! Ain't I right, Mr Dickers?"

When he failed to answer, Gerard grabbed him by the collar and pulled him to his feet.

"I may be old, but I sure as heck ain't senile! Those men who burned down my cabin were Wicker's thugs. Sent to scare me off, or get rid of me outright! And you knew about it, didn't you?"

Fulford had turned as white as an undertaker's shirt. He tried to speak, but no words escaped his open mouth. Gerard carried on, eyeballing him nose to nose, spraying the terrified bank manager with flecks of spittle.

"Let me tell *you* what happened," he hissed. "This buzzard Wicker wants the whole valley emptied, so he pays you to be his agent, to buy out all the sad fools who'd sell their grandmother's teeth for a few dollars! You make a tidy profit. But you don't bother telling me, do you? Why? Because you told Wicker that I had ignored your approaches and that the only way to get me to move was by sending in his thugs. That way, I'd be disposed of and you'd get your slimy hands on my gold! Am I right, Mr Dickers?" Gerard let go of the collar, letting Fulford drop like a sack of coal to the vault floor, where he began to sob incoherently.

Suddenly, there was the sound of a voice, a strident voice, from within the bank.

"Dickers! Is that you in there? Come out here, man!"

Gerard saw Fulford Dickers's eyes open wide with alarm. Judging by the terrified manager's reaction, he could guess who was speaking. He stepped out of the vault, crowbar still in hand.

Standing in the light of the open door was the figure of a burly man, his shoulders thrust back in the manner of someone who commands respect and fear in equal measure. He was a vision in white: white suit and shirt, white hair and moustache; even his teeth glowed an unnatural white. A blood red tie, precisely knotted at his throat, was all that broke the blinding purity of the picture.

It was Samuel Z Wicker III.

"Where's that fool Dickers? And who on earth are you?" he boomed, catching sight of Gerard.

Gerard stood his ground, carefully eyeing the burly tycoon like a bear sniffing the air for danger.

"My name is Tarras. Gerard Tarras. But I'd wager you already know that."

If the Great Man was startled, he certainly didn't show it, but something reptilian flickered deep in his eyes.

"Ahh! Mr Tarras. The hermit palaeontologist!" he barked, stepping over the debris on the floor, extending a manicured hand.

Gerard was taken aback. "I won't be shaking hands with the man who tried to have me killed!"

The Great Man withdrew his hand and laughed. "Believe me, Mr Tarras, if I wanted you dead, you would be very dead right now. I was actually hoping to talk with you, as it happens."

Gerard continued to eye the tycoon suspiciously. "Burning my cabin . . . my life's work. That's a strange way to open a discussion!" he said angrily.

The Great Man snorted and brushed a fleck of dust from his white cuff.

"The burning of your cabin was regrettable. That fool Dickers got greedy." He looked past Gerard to the quivering figure of the bank manager, still huddled in the vault. "But I'm assuming you were just discussing that with him when I arrived," he said with a thin smile. "I was hoping to chat with you about your research."

Gerard was taken aback. "My research?"

"Yes. Your theory about Captain Ezra Bellevue's creature of the lake."

Now Gerard was completely stunned. "How did you know about that?"

Samuel Z flashed a crocodilian smile, his dazzling teeth gleaming in the dusty sunlight. "I make it my business to know such things." He reached into his pocket and produced a worn leather book. "And I am an avid reader as well." The smile had left his lips.

Gerard stared in disbelief at the book in the tycoon's hand. It was Captain Bellevue's journal!

"You swine!" shouted Gerard, leaping forward to snatch the precious book. "That belongs to me!"

Suddenly, Gerard felt a blow to the back of his head, opening the old wound with a brief stab of excruciating pain before he slumped to the floor unconscious.

"Glad to see you're of some use after all, Dickers," Samuel Z sneered. "Now get out of my sight!"

The bank manager dropped the metal deposit box he'd used to club Gerard and scurried out the door like a rat released from a trap.

When he came to, Gerard found himself bound hand and foot to a wooden chair inside the vault. It was late in the afternoon; long, cold shadows crawled across the floor.

Samuel Z was seated by the vault's metal door. He had a camp table set up beside him, and a rake-thin manservant was pouring coffee into a white china cup.

Careful not to disturb his manicured moustache, he sipped from the cup and eyed the dazed old man dispassionately.

"I'd offer you a coffee, Tarras, but I suspect you'd have difficulty holding the cup."

Gerard's eyes blazed. He struggled against the knots but they had been tied by an expert. "What do you want?" he demanded angrily.

Carefully, Samuel Z put down the china cup and dabbed his thick lips with the corner of the starched napkin proffered by his ever-watchful manservant.

"Oh, there are many things I want." His smile was sinister. "And I always end up getting them. Always." He reached into his breast pocket and withdrew Captain Bellevue's journal. "I wanted this, for instance, and now I have it. Simple."

"You got your thugs to steal it!" Gerard spat out the words, the veins in his neck bulging.

"Same result. Anyway, let's not quibble over how I got it. Let's talk about what is written within."

"You can read it for yourself, can't you?"

The Great Man's eyes became slits. "I can and I have . . . many times since it came into my possession yesterday. Very interesting reading, I must say. Some would think it to be no more than the deluded writing of a crazy man."

"You should know," sneered Gerard, wondering where this conversation was leading.

"They told me you were a feisty old fool." Samuel Z laughed mockingly, then stood suddenly and, with one stride, came within a centimetre of Gerard's startled face. His eyes shone with the glint of madness.

"You find a skeleton on an island in the middle of a god-forsaken lake with an old journal beside it, and you think you've discovered a secret. The lake contains a mythological beast! A giant man-eating eel!

"You spend a lifetime searching for proof of such a creature, become a hermit with a cabin full of bones and fossils, yet you are no closer to proving its existence today than you were the day you first read the crazed captain's scribblings. Fifty years wasted on a fool's dream!"

Gerard's eyes bulged but he said not a word. The man had summed up his pitiful life in a mere minute and he knew it. Fifty years of fruitless searching, with nothing to show for it.

Samuel Z could read in the old man's eyes what his tongue would never admit. He had spent his own lifetime divining men's minds and dissecting their intentions.

He returned to his chair and flicked open the leather journal, lost in thought, while the old man watched, slumped in his bonds. When he finally put down the book and spoke, the Great Man's words were like a bucket of ice water thrown in Gerard's face.

"The fact is, Gerard Tarras, I believe every word written in this journal. And, what's more, I believe I've found the creature you've been looking for!"

Gerard stared at him, eyes wide open in shock, heart pounding so hard it almost burst through his chest. In spite of his bonds, he was suddenly desperate to know more. Yet how could he be sure the Great Man wasn't just toying with him?

"You expect me to believe you? Untie me then and prove it!" he demanded.

Samuel Z laughed, then snapped his fingers.

"Do I expect you to believe me? No. But I have something to show you that will prove very hard for you to disbelieve. Manolo! The photographs, if you please!"

The servant disappeared back into the bank and returned quickly with a large leather bag. He snapped open the clips and removed a manila folder, handing it to his master with a precisely executed bow, his black eyes unblinking.

"Excellent!" crowed Samuel Z as he fanned a series of large black and white photographs in his thick fingers, like an oversized pack of cards. "The detail is astonishing. Would you care to see for yourself, Mr Tarras?"

He arranged them on the floor in front of Gerard's feet and the old man craned forward to see them, squinting in the fading shaft of afternoon light.

"Bring a light for our friend!" snapped Samuel Z, sending Manolo scurrying away once more.

The servant returned with a kerosene lamp and placed it on the floor, where it cast a yellow light on the fanned photographs.

Gerard gasped out loud. For a full five minutes

he was struck speechless. Nothing he had seen in all his seventy years had prepared him for these images. Not even his wildest dreams.

There were a dozen glossy photographs. Each one was of the same subject, but taken from a slightly different angle. The detail was stunning.

They all depicted a creature, black and shiny, moving through dark water, a trail of foam in its wake. Its eyes were black – large and seemingly devoid of life. A slash of a mouth revealed rows of glistening, razor-sharp teeth. Yet it was the size of the creature that was most stunning. Gerard guessed it to be more than twenty metres in length, and that was just the parts he could see on the surface! The images were at once terrifyingly strange but remarkably familiar.

It was an image Gerard had hoped to see every waking day for the past fifty years. His giant eel!

When words finally reached his tongue, his lips, parched and dry, could not form them properly.

"Get him water!" barked Samuel Z.

Manolo held a crystal tumbler of water to the old man's lips.

"Where did you get these?" Gerard gasped.

The Great Man bent down and scooped one of the photographs up in his stubby fingers. He toyed with it, holding it to the light.

"Wonderful, aren't they? One of my men took them. He was camping at the northern end of the lake, on a surveying job for my new dam. As chance would have it, he was also an avid amateur photographer. It was getting late and, with the light beginning to fade, he thought he'd take a panoramic view of the soon-to-be drowned lake and the Black River township. That's when he saw it. A movement in his lens, at first nothing more than a ripple on the dead calm lake. But, as he looked again, it became a foaming wake and there, breaking the surface, was the creature you see before you now. It would be a vast understatement to say he was stunned. When I spoke with him, he was still shaken and white as a corpse."

Samuel Z sat back, his splayed fingers propped together like a church steeple, a malevolent grin on his lips, watching the old man intently for his reaction.

Gerard took a long while to find any words to say. The photographs and the accompanying story had traumatised him. There was no denying their authenticity.

After all this time, here at his feet was the documentary proof of the object of his life's search.

Yet another question was forcing its way to the front of his mind.

"Why burn my cabin and steal the journal? Why do that if you have all the evidence you need?"

Samuel Z leaned forward, his nasty smile gone for the moment. "Because, old man, I needed to know for sure – needed to find out all I could about this creature. Needed to know who else had heard of it or even seen it. I made enquiries and found out that you, the crazy hermit of the hills, had been searching for a giant man-eating eel for half a century! They said you were a pathological fool, insane with your fantasies. I needed to find out for myself."

Gerard looked up at him. "So, now you have me here, hog-tied to this chair. Why? Just to show me these pictures? Just to rub my nose in them? Make fun of an old man?"

"Oh no. On the contrary. I wanted to know your opinion. In my line of work, I have learned always to seek expert opinion."

"You wanted my opinion?" cried Gerard in amazement. "You have in your hands photographic evidence of the single most amazing discovery of the century . . . a discovery that I have longed to make myself!"

Samuel Z Wicker's eyes blazed. "So, you agree! It is your opinion that what my surveyor saw and photographed is the creature from Captain Bellevue's journal. None other than a giant eel?"

"A creature of the Carboniferous period, certainly," said Gerard. "Unlike any such creature yet discovered – a monumental find! Of that I am certain."

"Excellent!" cried the Great Man. "That is exactly what I had hoped to hear. It ties up loose ends and I detest loose ends."

Gerard felt an icy chill run up his spine. The thumping pain in his head grew more insistent.

"You didn't need to tie me to a chair in this vault just to get my opinion, did you?"

"No."

"You don't intend to tell anyone about this discovery, do you?"

"Again, no."

"And I would guess the surveyor who took the photographs is no longer in your employ?"

"A tragic drowning."

"I suppose Black River will be a 'tragic drowning' as well?"

The Great Man paused, as if considering Gerard's question. When he finally answered, he seemed to be talking out loud to himself rather than to the old man bound to the chair. His eyes shone with a chilling madness.

"I have invested a considerable sum of money into creating my vision of a city, my Metropolene. When it is complete, it will rival the greatest cities in the world. I will bring it forth from the bare ground . . . and nothing will stop me – nothing! That is why I will drown this insignificant town and the lake and valley it squats in. I will drown it to create a giant hydro lake worthy of powering my Metropolene. When the dam is complete and the power begins to flow, my city will grow. People will flood to it. Buildings will bloom. I will become incalculably rich!" He stood, hands on hips, head thrust high, his nostrils flared like some wild bull in the ring. Then he turned to Gerard Tarras, his eyes still brimming with his fantasy.

"But! If word were to leak out about the discovery of a giant man-eating creature in my new lake, it would be disastrous. Disastrous! Who would wish to live by a lake, have their children play near water that was infested with a giant eel with a taste for flesh? Therefore, it must remain a secret, and all those who know of its existence must remain silent."

"The silence of the grave?" Gerard spat.

"There is no greater silence!"

"What about the giant eel – will you let it live?"

"That would be extremely foolhardy. I cannot risk its discovery – now or ever. Therefore I will have it found and disposed of immediately, even if I have to dynamite the whole lake myself!"

On hearing this, Gerard snapped. Still fully bound, he lunged at Samuel Z like a gored bull, head lowered in an enraged charge.

Leopard-like, Manolo sprang forward, dealing the old man a savage kick that sent him crashing, head first, into the brick wall of the vault.

Gerard lay motionless, blood trickling from the corner of his mouth, as Samuel Z poked him impassively with the toe of his shoe and then picked up the remaining photographs.

"It would seem that our job here is finished, Manolo."

He tossed Captain Bellevue's journal onto the floor by Gerard's unconscious body.

"We will not need this any more – or the old fool, either. Manolo, untie him, then seal the vault."

Chapter Seven

Josh buried the old man beneath a pile of wet bricks on the outskirts of Black River. It wasn't easy. Gerard Tarras's body, contorted in death, had hardened with rigor mortis. His arms remained outstretched, locked in place, as if still begging for justice.

Josh and Greer carried the body to its final resting place together. Twice she gagged and turned to retch and cough. Josh hadn't felt much better.

They had both agreed that they couldn't just leave the old man's remains to rot in the empty vault, especially now the sealed door that had preserved his body was smashed open.

It was Josh who suggested burying him above ground, beneath a cairn of bricks. Greer had fashioned a wooden cross out of some broken chair legs and bound them together with a bit of old rope she found on the floor.

They stood briefly by the grave, shivering. It was night by then and a cold wind was whipping off the black waters of the lake.

"Should we say something?" asked Greer, keen to head back to the shelter of the vault.

"I've only ever been to one funeral before," replied Josh. "My father's."

She turned to him, surprise in her eyes.

"Your father? I never knew. I mean, you never told me . . ." Her words trailed away in the darkness.

"It's okay. It happened a long time ago," said Josh, staring at the wooden cross thrust into the mud at the head of the grave.

He felt the warmth of her body beside him, her hand found his.

"How . . . how did he die?" She almost whispered the words.

Josh sighed, as if reaching deep for a buried memory.

"I was seven years old. Dad had taken me fishing. I'd been hassling him for ages to take me. I had a new rod for Christmas and was jumping out of my skin to try it out. So he borrowed a boat, a small runabout, and we headed out across the bay. He wasn't a fisherman; not much of a sailor, either, and he hadn't checked the forecast. Anyway, a huge storm front came out of nowhere and just dumped on us – rain and wind and waves as high as a house. Dad tried to turn our boat around and head back to shore, but the motor just wouldn't start. He tried for ages; all the time the boat was drifting and the waves were smashing over the side. A huge dumper knocked me off my feet and threw me overboard. I had a life jacket on but, even so, I was gulping sea water and floundering badly.

"I was screaming out for Dad, screaming. But the boat just drifted away in the storm . . . I never saw him again. Coastguard found me a couple of hours later, floating in the sea, semi-conscious. They never found Dad or the boat. I blamed myself for years . . ." Josh's voice trailed away.

"It wasn't your fault. You were only seven years old," said Greer, gripping his hand tightly.

"That's exactly what my mum used to say," he replied, still lost in his thoughts. "Funny thing is, I never went out in a boat again, ever. In fact, today was the first time I'd been in the water for so long. Hanging on to that log, thinking I was going to drown . . . I thought of Dad. Maybe he was looking after me, protecting me from that . . . thing."

Greer looped her arm around him. He felt her head resting on his shoulder, could smell her hair.

They said nothing for a while, just stood in the darkness together.

Josh thought back to the time he'd shown up at the Maranatha High School Hiking Club meeting. His motives were as murky then as the lake that surrounded him now. His only intention had been to get close to Greer.

Well, in spite of the horrors of the past two days, in spite of it all, he was closer to her now than he'd ever dreamed of.

Yet, at that same moment, Josh had never felt so perfectly alone in his entire life.

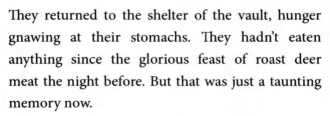

They returned to the shelter of the vault, hunger gnawing at their stomachs. They hadn't eaten anything since the glorious feast of roast deer meat the night before. But that was just a taunting memory now.

The one consolation had been the discovery of a kerosene lantern and a box of matches, taken gingerly from old Gerard's shirt pocket, as if the dead man might awake and object.

With these they at least had light. To take their minds off food, they read and reread the old man's testament and Captain Bellevue's journal by the flickering light – the dying words of two men separated by a century. Both their last thoughts were of the black creature of the lake.

Gerard Tarras had written his last testament of events in a looping, spidery hand that got progressively harder to decipher. But the events he recorded in his dying moments were still shockingly clear. He had been buried alive, deliberately left to asphyxiate in the sealed vault while the lake around him was flooded, drowning Black River and him with it.

How long he had survived before the air was used up, Josh and Greer could only guess. Long enough for him to have written his last account. Then he had died as they had found him, preserved like some ancient mummy.

Samuel Z Wicker III had hated loose ends. He had considered the old hermit to be a loose end. By sealing the old man in his underwater tomb and covering him with the cold, black depths of Lake Wicker, he had thought that loose end was permanently tied.

Chapter Seven

He was wrong.

Mt Darius had seen to that. The mighty dam had cracked and bled. Black River had risen from its watery grave and, with it, Gerard Tarras's secret.

"Murderer!" Greer cried as she read the old man's final words once more.

"He got away with it, though, didn't he?" said Josh. "Nobody missed Gerard Tarras while he lived, and I guess no one noticed when he was gone. Too late for justice now."

Greer picked up the journal. "Poor old Gerard. He was right after all. The giant eel *was* in the lake, just as he said it was for fifty years."

"Still is!" said Josh. "Obviously Wicker never did manage to find it and kill it. It's still alive."

She looked at him in the flickering light. "That's obviously what we saw today – the thing's been breeding, hasn't it?"

"It fits the description in the journal. Who knows how many of them there are, or how big."

"When that murderer Wicker flooded the valley and made his huge hydro lake, the eel must have grown in size," she said suddenly, her mind spinning with the implications of what she was thinking.

"What do you mean?" asked Josh.

"Like a fish in a tank. They only ever grow as large

as the environment that contains them. Put that same fish in a bigger tank and it'll grow accordingly! The giant eel must've done the same."

Josh's eyes widened. "Except now the lake has shrunk. That'll mean there's one big mother of an eel in one small lake!"

They huddled together beneath a canvas tarpaulin found among the jumble of empty crates and safety deposit boxes and stared into the light of the lantern until well into the night.

When sleep came, it was fitful.

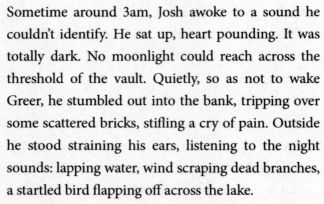

Sometime around 3am, Josh awoke to a sound he couldn't identify. He sat up, heart pounding. It was totally dark. No moonlight could reach across the threshold of the vault. Quietly, so as not to wake Greer, he stumbled out into the bank, tripping over some scattered bricks, stifling a cry of pain. Outside he stood straining his ears, listening to the night sounds: lapping water, wind scraping dead branches, a startled bird flapping off across the lake.

He heard no other sounds and concluded it must have been his dreams that woke him. Yet, as he turned to stumble back to the womb-like blackness of the vault, he heard something else.

It was coming from the lake. He could hear, muffled but distinctive, carried on the night air, a steady slosh of water. Instinctively, he crouched down, listening for it again. And there it was, moving closer, growing more audible.

Slosh, swish, slosh, swish . . .

It was the unmistakable sound of someone rowing a boat! Josh's mind raced. Every sinew of his body wanted to explode in shouts of welcome and waving of arms. Yet he stayed crouched, like a small animal sensing danger, sniffing the air.

The rowing stopped.

He heard nothing for a minute and wondered if it had been his sleep-starved imagination playing tricks on him.

He was just about to rise when he heard the sound of a boat being scraped along rocks, dragged up away from the water, then the hollow sound of oars being stowed. There was a crunch of footsteps on the stony shore, then silence, as if the mysterious rower were taking bearings, uncertain which way to go.

Suddenly, a light flared in the night. It was a storm lantern. Josh could hear it hissing from his hiding place behind the bricks.

Now he wanted to leap up and shout out. It must be rescuers, surely?

But it was as though a giant hand kept him crouched and hidden, watching. The outline of the rower could be seen in silhouette against the lantern light, face obscured by the glare. It was a man, that much Josh could determine. And, now that he was moving again, he could see he was lanky, walking with long, loping strides.

The mysterious figure came up from the shore and began stepping carefully over the muddy debris of the main street, heading straight towards the spot where Josh was hiding.

Now Josh could hear a sound behind him. It was Greer. She'd awoken to find him gone and had seen the glare of the rower's light bouncing off the bank walls. Now she emerged from the building, addled by sleep, eyes squinting at the approaching light.

"Josh? Is that you?" she called out, hand raised over her eyes.

Immediately, the rower stopped in his tracks. The light hissed out, leaving a faint orange glow that soon faded into darkness. Josh heard footsteps retreating back to the bay. He leapt up, almost knocking over a startled Greer, and raced off in the direction the rower had gone. He could hear the boat scraping back across the rocks, then the plunge of oars in the lake. He reached the water's edge, but the boat was gone. "Hey! Over here!" Josh called. "Come back! We're here . . . two of us!"

But, save for the slosh of water on the rocky shore, there was only silence. Josh slumped to his knees, cursing his indecision. Why had he waited so long to call out? Why hadn't he shouted out the moment he heard the rower approach? What a stupid fool! For two days they'd been praying for the sight of rescuers; now one arrives and what does he do – he hides in the rubble like a frightened deer! And now the rescuer was gone.

"Josh! *Josh!*" called Greer, emerging through the trees. "Where are you? What's going on? Who are you calling out to?"

He got to his feet and waved her over. "There was someone, a guy I think, in a boat . . ."

She seemed shocked – many different emotions flashed over her face in quick succession.

"A boat? They found us? We're going to get out of here!"

She ran to the lake edge, staggering over the rocks in her excitement, looking for the rescuers.

"Where are they, Josh? I can't see a thing. Where did you see him?"

"He's gone," Josh mumbled.

"Gone?" She whirled around, her eyes brimming with fiery tears.

"What do you mean gone? You said he was here a minute ago – I heard you calling to him! How could he be gone?"

"I heard a noise . . . someone on the lake. It woke me up. I came outside and saw a light, a lantern, heading towards me . . ."

"So you shouted out for help, right?"

He stumbled for the words. "No. I was going to . . . I really wanted to, but . . ."

"But what, Josh?"

"I can't explain it . . . It didn't feel right . . ."

Greer exploded, fuelled by anger and frustration.

"Didn't *feel right*? You let our only chance of being rescued row away because you 'didn't feel right' about it? Tom was right about you, Josh Brookfield. You haven't got a clue about anything! You should have stayed back on your couch, stuffing your face with chips. You're no use out here! No use at all!"

Josh was stunned by her angry words. All the more because he knew it was all true. What *was* he doing out here at all?

She pushed past him angrily and strode over the rocks and down to the lake edge, shouting out across the black water. "Can you hear me? I'm Greer Machon! We're trapped on this island!" She went on shouting for some time, her voice steadily becoming more hoarse.

In a final act of frustration, she waded waist-deep into the lake, pounding the dark water with her fists, tears streaming down her cheeks. "Will somebody help us?"

Josh felt so helpless watching her. Helpless and hopeless and useless. He squatted on the rocks, fighting the tears that were damming up behind his eyes. Why had the rower disappeared so suddenly? He must've heard them call out. Why turn off his light and row away? It just didn't make any sense. He peered out over the black water.

Greer was still pounding the lake in bitter frustration.

Suddenly, something caught his eye. A movement, fast and fluid, on the surface of the lake, no more than thirty metres away. He sprang to his feet, frantically running down to the shoreline. "Greer! Get back! Get back!"

She turned, startled.

He was running now, as best he could on the sharp rocks, and pointing out to the lake.

Heading straight towards Greer, its serpentine

undulations marked out by a phosphorescent wake, was the creature of Captain Bellevue's nightmares. Its black neck and head cut a path through the inky water.

Staggering back in terror, Greer stumbled on a rock and tumbled into the water. Josh scooped up a jagged rock and sprinted for the place she'd fallen. He heaved the rock at the approaching eel.

It rose out of the water with such force that Josh froze in stunned horror. He could see its huge, gaping mouth – a black hole lined with fearsome teeth. The eel reared back, mouth agape, poised to strike at Greer, to tear her apart with those deadly razor-sharp teeth.

With every last bit of strength he possessed, Josh hurled himself at Greer, tackling her around the waist, driving them both up onto the rocky shore.

The giant eel's mighty head crashed down within centimetres of Josh's back – so close he could smell the stench of its breath. Then it turned and dropped back into the water as swiftly as it had come.

Josh dragged Greer higher up the shoreline and together they huddled in the lee of the trees, not moving, not saying a word, until the first rays of sunlight seeped over the surrounding black hills.

Chapter Eight

The following day arrived with dazzling sunshine. The ash clouds and dark, brooding skies were gone and the wind had dropped to nothing more than a baby's breath. Even the lake seemed to sparkle.

Greer lay silently on the warm rocks, soaking up the morning sun, while Josh headed back towards the vault to retrieve the box of matches and some dry wood for a fire. They were both weak from hunger, and the trauma of the previous night still hung heavy over them. Greer hadn't spoken a word since he'd dragged her out of the water. Yet, somehow, in the warm spring sunshine, Josh felt a renewed hope.

Whoever the strange rower was, at least there

were other humans in the vicinity, and that meant rescue could be imminent.

As he walked back along the lakeshore, he came across something on the rocks that hadn't been there the previous evening. He stepped over to examine it more closely.

It was a sack, rough and knotted at the throat. It looked as if it had been deliberately placed there. He whirled around, expecting to see someone nearby, but there was no one.

Gingerly, he lifted the sack. It was heavy and bulging. He untied the knot and, as the contents spilled out, he staggered back in shock.

It was food!

There were tins of sardines, a bag of rice, a small wheel of cheese wrapped in cloth, a cob of bread, crusty and pungent. There was also a can opener, a small billy and some tea bags.

Josh scooped it all back into the sack hurriedly, as if someone might suddenly emerge and take the food away again. Then he sprinted back to Greer.

He had no idea where the food sack had come from. And, at that moment, he didn't care.

Greer's reaction to his discovery was equally stunned. She still wasn't speaking, but her eyes widened in amazement as he revealed the sack's contents. It was no time for questions.

Hungrily, they pounced on the cheese and bread, stuffing their mouths till their jaws ached. Then they ripped open the sardine tins, consuming the oily fish whole, like seals at feeding time. His belly pleasantly full, Josh built a fire, filled the billy from the lake and boiled the rice.

Soon they were gorging on white, fluffy rice, scooping it from the hot billy with their fingers, dipping it in the remains of the oily sardines.

Afterwards, Josh cleaned the billy and boiled more water for tea. He was watching it bubble and brew when Greer finally spoke.

"Josh," she said hesitantly, "I'm sorry."

"For what?" he replied, stirring the tea.

"For the way I spoke to you – for calling you useless . . ."

"Forget it. You were right. I *am* kind of useless."

Her eyes flashed and she stepped over to the spot where he sat and took his hands in hers.

"You saved my life last night, Josh Brookfield." Then, to his astonishment, she leaned forward and kissed him on the cheek.

Before he had time to respond, she had returned to her place in the sun. "So, who left the food?" she asked, as if the kiss had never happened.

"Must've been the rower," Josh replied, trying to stop his face from turning the colour of boiled beetroot.

"Strange that he didn't want to be seen, though. I mean, why all the secrecy? Why leave the food like that?"

But Josh wasn't listening. He was staring out over the sun-dappled lake.

Dead logs still dotted the surface and the far side was dark with shadow, but there was something moving towards them.

Greer stopped talking as she noticed Josh's worried look.

"Is it the eel?"

"No. Don't think so at least. Look, over on the far shore, do you see it?"

She stood and looked, shading her eyes against the bright sunlight.

Against the far shore, almost hidden in the overhanging shadows, something was moving.

"It's a boat. A dinghy of some sort," she said.

"The rower?"

"Must be, and he's headed this way."

They watched in silence as the boat emerged from the shadows on the far side of the lake and slowly, methodically, made its way across the water.

When it entered a pool of sunshine, they could make out its single occupant, bent over the oars, rowing with deliberate strokes. The dinghy was old and battered and Josh was sure the person rowing it was the same man he'd seen the previous evening. He was tall and thin, his knees almost touching his chin as he leaned forward with each stroke. A large-brimmed hat obscured his face, but they could see that he wore a badly stained jacket of calico and old baggy trousers of the same material. He rowed slowly, expertly avoiding the floating logs.

When he was about six metres offshore, his back to them, Greer called out.

"Are we glad to see you. Thanks for the food!"

The rower stopped rowing, set down his oars and turned to look at them.

He was an old man, with skin like oiled mahogany, etched with deep creases and scars. He said nothing but motioned, with a bony finger to his lips, for them to be quiet.

For a long time, he just sat in the boat, drifting in the gentle current, saying not a word.

Greer and Josh had no idea what he was up to. Yet they stood obediently still by the lake edge, waiting for him to make a move.

Then, suddenly, the old man picked up the

oars and resumed rowing. When his boat bumped against the rocky shore, he beckoned them urgently to him.

Greer was about to speak again, but he made the same "be quiet" motion with his finger, pointing with his other hand to the water of the lake.

Then, still wordless, he directed them into the dinghy, indicating that Greer should sit in the stern and Josh at the bow.

They hesitated at first, unsure about embarking on the lake, both still shaken by the events of the previous night. Greer was visibly trembling when she eventually clambered into the boat.

Seated in the bow, Josh kept his hands away from the edge of the boat and imagined that every floating log must be the eel waiting out there in the water.

The old man pushed the boat away from the shore, climbed in after them and began rowing out into the lake with the same deft oar strokes that Josh had heard last night – rhythmic and almost hypnotic . . . slosh, swish . . . slosh, swish.

He rowed in silence and, despite their fears, Josh and Greer were soon calmed by the steady motion of the oars.

The lake sparkled uncharacteristically and there was no sign of any creature, save the occasional startled mallard flapping away as they rowed by.

Occasionally, Josh caught Greer's eye over the old man's shoulder. She gave him a what-the-heck-is-going-on look and he shrugged his shoulders silently. The old man had never made eye contact with him, and he didn't look now at Greer, even though their knees were almost touching in the cramped boat. And every time he leant back at the end of an oar stroke, Josh could smell him. It was a musty, almost feral smell, with whiffs of wood smoke and hay. Josh watched the old man's back as he rowed. His hands and arms were dark and sinewy, richly veined and his silver hair was pulled back under his hat in a tight ponytail.

He also saw a hessian sack in the bottom of the boat – the same kind as the one in which the food had been stashed. There was a storm lantern next to it. And, more troubling, a double-barrelled shotgun.

They were now on a part of the lake they had not seen before. The island and town of Black River were some distance away, a dark smear on the lake, with just the poignant remains of crumbling buildings poking above the ragged tree line.

The old man continued rowing into the cool shadows hugging the lake edge, where the dank foliage drooped so low they frequently had to duck their heads.

It was midday when they finally arrived at a well-hidden inlet. Steep cliffs rose up on each side, casting dark shadows over the water.

Josh and Greer stared in amazement. At the end of the inlet was a concrete jetty, green with slime and almost black with age. But they could clearly see a series of steps leading up from the water.

The old man guided the dinghy to the steps and hurled a rope expertly up onto the jetty and around a rusty bollard. He motioned Josh to get out first and then he followed, turning to assist Greer as the boat bobbed unevenly in the water. He retrieved his sack and rifle and nimbly climbed the steep steps, beckoning them to follow.

They did as he indicated, glad to be away from the lake and the island, but unsure where their strange rescuer was leading them. The steps had been excavated out of the side of a cliff and, on the exposed side, they plunged straight down to the dark inlet below.

"Where are we going?" whispered Greer.

"Up," gasped Josh, the exertion robbing him of breath.

"Do you think he could be mute or something?"

"Maybe."

"How do we know if we can trust him?"

"Got a better plan?"

At last the cliff steps ended and they began climbing a steeply forested hill. The vegetation seemed to have escaped the effects of the eruption, and pine trees, pungent and damp, cast their cool shadows over them. Birds were actually singing and the air was fresh and moist.

At the summit, the trees gave way to a rocky outcrop and they rested in the sun for a moment, speechless from the exertion of the climb, but also at the sight that greeted them. In a panoramic sweep, they could see the lake below, a small black heart of water set amid a barren valley. They could trace the Black River as it ran from the lake through the hills until it reached . . .

"The Wicker Dam!" cried Greer, pointing to the huge concrete structure that lay below them.

"Or what's left of it," Josh added, stunned at the destruction wrought by the earthquake.

The mighty dam lay between two enormous peaks, stretching across the river in a swathe of concrete and steel. At its centre, it had collapsed like a child's sandcastle, opening up a giant chasm through which a surge of water still thundered.

"No wonder Lake Wicker emptied so fast!" Josh

said with a whistle.

But Greer was looking back to the little island and the town of Black River, away in the distance.

"Do you remember what old Gerard Tarras called the lake, before it was flooded, before it got named Wicker? It was in his last testament . . . something in Portuguese?"

Suddenly, the old man removed his hat and wiped the sweat from his dark brow. Then, to Greer and Josh's astonishment, he spoke.

"The Portuguese called that lake Lago da Morte. It means Lake of the Dead." He stood, arched his back and stretched, then beckoned them both, still wide-eyed with surprise, to follow him.

"Come, now I will take you to Lake House."

Chapter Nine

Samuel Z Wicker III had begun work on Lake House the same day the dam construction started. It was to be his sumptuous mountaintop residence, boasting stunning panoramic views of the mighty dam, Lake Wicker and beyond to where his beloved Metropolene would rise from the forest.

He had spared no expense in its creation. Labourers and craftsmen toiled like slaves to complete it on schedule. The Great Man wanted to be in residence within the year and would brook no compromise or slacking. He whipped the workers with his fiery tongue and on many occasions with his buckled belt.

So Lake House rose swiftly from the ground,

transforming itself into a towering edifice, four storeys high, of stunning Italian marble and expensive granite. Its huge gabled roof boasted fifty chimneys, allowing every room a lavish fireplace, and crystal chandeliers dripped from every ceiling.

The furnishings had cost the Great Man a king's ransom. There were ornate chairs and settees upholstered in the richest brocades, drapes of the finest velvet, four-poster beds intricately carved and luxuriously canopied.

His study alone was the size of a ballroom, with a massive oak desk at its centre, complete with carved eagle-feet legs and burnished leather top.

A giant wall of books lined one side and the other was taken up with a mammoth floor-to-ceiling window with views of the ant-like construction of the Wicker Dam below. From a gargantuan leather chair, Samuel Z, cigar in hand, watched the workmen's progress, barking an incessant stream of invective and orders to the ever-hovering Manolo.

Yet, aside from Manolo and a bevy of cooks and household servants, Lake House was empty. Its fifty rooms were vacant, like those of a grand hotel in winter. The Great Man had never contemplated marriage and mistrusted what few family members he had. In fact, Manolo and his young wife Maria were the only "family" who lived in the echoing mansion, though they slept in the cramped servants' quarters above the stables.

The workers who dared to pause from their labour below and look up at the fabulous mansion could only wonder at the wealth that had built it.

Only Manolo knew the terrible truth. It was a truth that lurked like dry rot at the foundations of Lake House and the extravagant lifestyle it appeared to boast of.

Samuel Z Wicker III, the Great Man, the Mighty Tycoon, was on the edge of complete bankruptcy! His vast fortune had been expended on the mammoth construction of the Wicker Dam, and it had swallowed up his wealth like an ocean of quicksand.

In his race to build the mighty dam and bring power to his dream city, he had uncharacteristically overlooked a detail of crushing significance. Mt Darius.

Even then, the mountain had shown signs of its volcanic bad temper. Experts had warned him not to build so big a dam so close to the unpredictable volcano. Yet he had bulldozed over their warnings and blasted them for trying to halt his frenzied construction. When they persisted in raising their concerns in the press, he had resorted to blackmail, bribery and, in one case, cold-blooded murder.

At last, he thought he had silenced his critics, and he proclaimed to the world that the Wicker Dam would be constructed to last for a millennium or more.

Six months into the construction, Mt Darius said otherwise. One midnight, a sizeable earth tremor rocked the Bellevue Forest, causing the newly poured concrete on the dam to crack alarmingly. Fissures opened up that were big enough to poke a fist into.

Samuel Z ordered the fissures and the cracks to be plastered over immediately and news of the damage never reached the press. But the workers whispered among themselves and their families and soon rumours spread.

Investors in the proposed city of Metropolene quit the project as quickly as they had come. "No one will live in a city underneath a leaky dam!" they cried. "One good shake and the whole thing will come down like a pack of cards!"

While they were pocketing their money, Samuel Z was forced to dig into his.

Without much-needed investors' capital, he was forking out money like hay – staggering amounts of cash – just to keep his fanatical dreams alive.

To win back investor confidence and prove to the world that his dam was quakeproof, he ordered, and paid for dearly, triple the usual amount of concrete and steel reinforcing to brace the gigantic dam.

Then, with his finances stretched to breaking point, the worst winter in living memory brought severe snowstorms, which halted the construction, already behind schedule, for three whole months. Wages for his five thousand-strong workforce were due, and that pushed the Great Man to the brink of bankruptcy.

Not that anyone would know. To the world he showed calm determination in the face of rumours and setbacks.

Only Manolo saw the other dark and terrible side. Alone in his giant study at night, the Great Man would drink himself almost insensible. Then he would rant and rave into the small hours, striding up and down, yelling at shadows, often smashing everything within reach, hurling books, piles of plans and crystal glasses into the blazing fire in fits of blind rage.

Manolo would enter the lion's den with a trembling heart and often took the brunt of the Great Man's fury. The dinner he bore on a silver tray would be hurled back in his face and, on more than one occasion, Samuel Z had grabbed him by the throat and threatened to "wring his neck" if news of his financial woes ever leaked out.

The end had come swiftly. One cold winter's day, two years into the dam's construction, the banks refused to honour Samuel Z Wicker's cheques. He had simply run out of money. Not a single cent was left; the cupboard of his once overwhelming fortune was bare. On that same day, hearing the news of his bankrupt state, the workforce downed tools and departed, leaving the great dam and its recently created lake to the wind and rain. No turbines would ever turn, not one watt of power would ever be generated.

Overnight, the most celebrated tycoon of the era became a bankrupt pariah, shunned by all. His dream city had turned into a nightmare. Only Manolo and Maria stayed when all the other servants departed Lake House like rats from a sinking ship.

Despite his gross mistreatment at the hands of the once Great Man, Manolo had nowhere else to go. His life had been spent in the service of his master, from the goldfields of St Lima to the mountains of the Bellevue. His fate had always been bound up with Samuel Z Wicker's. He also shared his master's dirty secrets – so many, even he had trouble remembering them all. All but one.

And that was the cold-hearted murder of old Gerard Tarras, now sealed in his watery tomb beneath Lake Wicker. Of all the terrible things Manolo had witnessed, and been an accomplice to, this had been the knife to his heart. It had penetrated his leaden conscience like no other. And there had been other moments of cruelty and horror. It was Manolo who, on his master's orders, shot Butch Tibbins in the back six times.

Yet, sealing the vault and leaving an innocent old man to die of suffocation as the waters of Lake Wicker rose around him – that was a guilty burden he would take to his grave. And so . . . he felt it was safer to stay with Samuel Z and ensure that the secrets never escaped than to leave with the others.

The Great Man never acknowledged Manolo's presence. His mind simply snapped. Like a spring tightened to an unbearable intensity, his brain suddenly and explosively unravelled.

It happened on the day that work on the dam ceased. Gasping with rage, spittle flying from his lips, he had raced down to the empty work site in white suit and tie and, with wild eyes, began hammering away with pick and shovel as though he were a dozen men.

"I don't need them!" he'd shouted. "I'll build it myself!"

All day his frenzied activity went on, leaving his manicured hands ripped open to the bone and bleeding profusely.

It took all of Manolo's sinewy strength to stop him from carrying on into the night. Somehow, he managed to drag and cajole him back to the house.

The weeks that followed were like a nightmare. With no money, no power, no food, Manolo was forced to hunt and fish, cooking over open fires by candlelight, hauling fresh water from the lake.

Samuel Z refused all food, roaming the empty rooms, ranting to his demons, smashing furniture, slashing paintings, burning books.

The once great manor began to slip into chaos. Over the years that followed, the Bellevue forest insidiously swallowed Lake House whole.

Josh saw it first. As he trudged behind the old man, his eyes lifted from the stony trail. In the gloom and shadows of the dense forest that surrounded them, he could make out a man-made structure, a ruin of tumbled stone.

Pine trees pressed in on the ruins from every side, and a thick veil of strangler vines almost obscured it from view. Yet it was still possible to tell it had once been a huge house of magnificent proportions.

Here and there a window could be seen, sprouting cancerous clumps of weeds, and ruptured chimney stacks poked up through the forest, choked with vines.

"This is Lake House?" asked Josh incredulously.

The old man nodded. "What remains of it," he said, disappearing along a narrow trail that ran down the side of the dark ruin. They followed after him, eyes adjusting to the gloom.

The trail led behind the house to a large cobbled yard, knee-high in weeds and jumbled debris: moss-covered bricks, rotting piles of timber and, strangely, the rusted hulk of an ancient motor car, its wooden-framed wheels long rotted away.

Behind this overgrown courtyard stood a stable building, surprisingly intact. The old man swung open a large wooden door and they followed him inside. The smell of old hay hit their nostrils first, rich and pungent, then the distinct smell of something cooking. It was coming from a room at the back of the barn.

When the old man opened the door to this compact room, they gasped at what they saw. The room's furnishings were practical enough. There was a bed against one wall and a table in the centre. An open fireplace dominated another wall, surrounded by cooking utensils and large cast-iron pots. A delicious aroma wafted out into the room from one of these pots, strung over a gently crackling fire.

It was the nature of the furnishings that had startled them. Although much faded and worn, the chairs, bed and table were all constructed from the finest materials and elaborately designed. Even the curtains that hung over the large stable windows were made of the richest, if faded, velvet. It all seemed so out of place in this humble dwelling.

Suddenly, another door to the side of the room squeaked open and in stepped an old lady, her hair pulled back in a tight bun, her skin the colour of coffee beans. Her eyes sparkled at the sight of Greer and Josh.

"Welcome to Lake House," she said in a voice as soft as sand in an hourglass. "You must be starving. Come, eat."

She sat them down at the table and, though they had a thousand questions racing through their minds, they hungrily ate the delicious stew she poured into their bowls. Freshly baked bread materialised and the smell was almost intoxicating. The old man ate alongside them, still silent, while the old lady busied herself with second helpings.

When they had eaten all they could eat, and were warmed from the inside out, they both began to talk at once.

"What is this place?"

"How did you find us on the island?"

"Have you alerted the authorities?"

The old lady raised her hand with a smile. "Please, one at a time. It has been a long while since my brother and I have had company." She turned to the old man and asked him in Spanish, "¿Qué les ha dicho usted?"

In reply, he simply shrugged and shook his head.

She gave him an admonishing look, then turned to Josh and Greer apologetically. "You must forgive my brother Carlos. He is, as I'm sure you have guessed, a man of few words. My name is Juanita and you are welcome here in our humble home. With regard to your questions, let me try to answer. This place was once the home of a wealthy man who died a long while ago. Our father, rest his soul, was his servant . . ."

"Was your father named Manolo?" interrupted Greer.

Both Juanita and Carlos gasped at the mention of the name.

"Yes! But how could you possibly know that?" Juanita asked, her dark eyes wide with amazement.

Greer told them of the discovery of old Gerard Tarras's body and the hand-written testament he had left in the vault of the Black River Bank.

"He mentioned Manolo in the note. Said he was the servant of Samuel Z Wicker III. Is this Wicker's house?"

"Si. It was. Now it is as empty as all his schemes. May he rot." Carlos spat into the fire.

"You must forgive my brother. Though he died long before we were born, we have lived in the shadow of Samuel Z Wicker all our lives. Our father was badly treated by him, but he refused to leave this house after Wicker's death. We were raised in these ruins and buried our beloved parents in this ground.

"We refused to live in his big house, and simply brought what furniture we could salvage here to the stable. You must believe us when we say, we have no love for Samuel Z Wicker!"

"None!" Carlos spat again.

"Did you know about the old hermit, Gerard Tarras? Did your father, Manolo, tell you about him?" Greer asked.

Juanita's eyes grew sad. She seemed to slump at the mention of the name.

"Our father never mentioned him directly to us, but we heard him whispering to our mother, Maria, late in the night about what had happened. It haunted him all his life. He was no saint, our father, yet he begged forgiveness in many a nightmare for his part in the death of the hermit. He would never venture onto the lake near the place where Black River town was drowned. This we witnessed, but never knew the whole truth of it. He took his guilt and his secret to the grave. We carried on living here in the stables. And now the secrets of the past are giving way to the present.

"Three days ago, when Mt Darius erupted, we awoke to find the dam had burst and Lake Wicker emptied. We could not believe our eyes when we saw that the town of Black River had re-emerged!

"Carlos was determined to row out to the island and see for himself if there was any evidence of the death of Gerard Tarras and finally put to rest the suspicions we had harboured all these years."

"That's when you stumbled on us?" asked Josh.

Carlos nodded by the fire, looking somewhat sheepish.

"Si. It was night. I rowed ashore to a ghost town and heard your voices. My reaction was to panic. I thought it was ghosts of the past on the Lake of the Dead. I fled, rowing for my life!"

Juanita laughed out loud.

"I told him he was an old fool! 'Go back!' I told him. I knew it must be the young ones the authorities were looking for . . ."

She saw their startled faces.

"We have a battery-powered radio. We heard news about the eruption and the search for a missing school hiking party. They mentioned five in the group. Are there others?"

Greer looked up suddenly and caught Josh's eye. "They're all dead," she said, fighting back the tears. "We had to leave them on the slopes of Mt Darius."

"If you hadn't found us on the island, we'd be the same," Josh added, and then looked at Carlos as if something was troubling him.

"What did you call the lake – the old Portuguese name?"

"'Lago da Morte . . . Lake of the Dead."

"Did your father tell you why it was called that?"

Carlos stared into the fire, poking the embers

with a piece of wood. Eventually he spoke, yet his eyes never left the fire.

"The Portuguese explorers found something evil in the lake."

"Evil like a creature? A giant eel?" Josh asked.

"Si! Espirito mau – an evil spirit they called it."

"Have you seen it?"

Carlos's black eyes flared. "I have never seen it and nor do I ever wish to see it! It is pure evil. I know the old hermit had seen it."

"No, he died without having seen it first-hand. But we've seen it – Greer and I. It tried to kill us, at least twice!"

Josh described what had happened to them, with Greer chipping in.

"¡Por Dios!" gasped Juanita. "It is true! We have heard only what our father told us. Much of this we thought was the ramblings of an old man. He would never go down to the lake without taking a loaded shotgun, as if he were fearful that the creature of his nightmares might come for him."

"Did he ever see it?" Greer asked.

"Not that he ever told us," Carlos answered. "Lake Wicker was vast and huge. Deep as well. A creature like the one you saw could spend a lifetime in such water and never be seen. I myself always look over my shoulder when I am on that lake. I always carry a loaded gun and keep my silence. My father left me nothing of value, just his fears."

Greer reached into the hessian sack, which she had carried from the island.

"You may want to read this then. It's Captain Ezra Bellevue's journal. We found it next to Gerard Tarras in the vault where he died. The creature he witnessed was the same one we saw, or its offspring at least. I suppose, now that the lake has shrunk, it is harder for it to hide."

"It isn't trying very hard to hide!" Josh said. "It came right for us!"

"Hunger," said Carlos. "The creature was probably driven by hunger. With the lake so much smaller, its food stocks will be low. Perhaps it will follow the Black River out to the ocean."

Greer shivered at the thought. "How large will it grow there?"

Josh reached for her hand. "That's not our worry right now. We'll be out of here as soon as we can tell someone where we are."

He turned to Carlos and Juanita. "Exactly how do we call for help out here? I don't suppose you guys have a phone or anything like that?"

Juanita shook her head. "No. The only way to get

help is on foot. Carlos will leave first thing in the morning. It will take him a day's walk to get to a forest ranger's hut. There is a two-way emergency radio there."

Josh offered to go with him but Carlos flatly refused. "You are still very weak from your ordeal. Better to rest. Help will arrive when it arrives, my young friend."

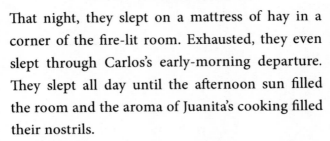

That night, they slept on a mattress of hay in a corner of the fire-lit room. Exhausted, they even slept through Carlos's early-morning departure. They slept all day until the afternoon sun filled the room and the aroma of Juanita's cooking filled their nostrils.

After generous servings of hearty vegetable soup, they were keen to stretch their legs and explore the ruins of Lake House. Juanita unlocked the door at the rear with a large, rusty key.

Inside it was dank and cold. Shafts of late-afternoon light streamed through huge gaps in the ceiling, lighting up the tumbled walls and smashed furniture within. Vines had infiltrated the walls and floors, wrapping their sinewy tentacles around everything in their path.

Together, Josh and Greer poked around the ruined rooms, stepping over smashed glass and the collected detritus of a century. Rats scurried across their path and nesting birds suddenly flapped away as they passed by.

With the light fading, Josh discovered the study and gasped. Looming down on them from the mouldy wall by the abandoned fireplace was Samuel Z Wicker III. Or his painted likeness, at least. White suit, blood red tie. Eyes tinged with mad desire.

"We meet at last," joked Josh, with a mock bow.

"Quite a guy!" said Greer, studying the painting. "Hard to imagine him as the murderer of poor old Gerard Tarras."

"Wonder whatever happened to him?" mused Josh, poking about in the ruins of the huge study.

Juanita had appeared at the study doorway, her eyes also drawn to the portrait of her father's former master. "No one knows. My father would never say anything more than that the Great Man went mad and drowned."

"Sounds like justice to me," said Greer, looking up at the mouldy portrait.

"Sounds like something else!" Josh exclaimed, running to the huge, glassless study window.

Chapter Nine

They all strained to hear.

Across the ruins of the once mighty Wicker Dam came the unmistakable whop-whop-whop of helicopter blades.

Greer's face dissolved in tears as she watched the chopper swooping in. Josh hesitated for a moment, and then knew exactly what to do. He leaned towards her and gently put his arm around her.

Epilogue

Samuel Z Wicker had stumbled down the sweeping steps of Lake House and staggered out over the lawn towards the lake.

He clutched a decanter of brandy in one hand and a double-barrelled shotgun in the other. He was raving drunk and raving mad.

"Manolo! Manolo, you stinking rat. It's all your fault! You told them, didn't you? Didn't you?"

Manolo lingered by the steps uncertainly.

"No, señor! No! I swear I said nothing to anybody!"

A gunshot exploded into the night air, narrowly missing the servant's head.

"You've ruined me, Manolo! I swear I'll kill you.

Do you hear me?"

Another gunshot.

Ducking for cover, Manolo ran, bent in half, along the low stone wall that ran down to the lake. He paused for breath, listening.

Samuel Z was fumbling with the ropes of a rowboat down at the jetty.

"I'll kill you and then I'll kill that beast – myself!" he shouted as he fell into the boat, almost swamping it. With difficulty, he rowed away from the jetty and out onto the lake, still cursing and threatening every shadow he saw.

Manolo watched his mad midnight row in the moonlight. He looked back at Lake House. It was as lifeless as a tomb. Empty windows stared back like dark eye sockets. But there was nothing to fear in that direction. He knew Maria would be safe in the stable.

When he turned back to the lake, he saw something out of the corner of his eye. It was moving at speed towards Samuel Z Wicker's boat. Instantly, Manolo recognised it from the ghastly photographs he had seen. It was the creature of the lake.

"Espirito mau!" he gasped.

Years of blind servitude to his master had conditioned him to react in the way he did now.

Ignoring his own safety, he raced along the edge of the lake, shouting, "Señor! It is the creature! The hermit's eel!"

Samuel Z looked up, startled. His drunken eyes focused on Manolo, screaming from the jetty. "There you are, you turncoat! So help me, I'll send you to your grave!"

Raising his shotgun, he fired both barrels at once and the blast sent him staggering back over the gunwales of the small boat. Manolo watched in horror as the Great Man landed with a thunderous splash in the water.

Suddenly, the giant eel breached the surface, its ugly head and dead eyes rising up with startling speed. And then the gaping mouth descended on the helpless Samuel Z, snatching him up in its razor-toothed jaws.

Manolo dropped to his knees, stunned and too terrified to speak. He watched in horror as the eel crushed his master in its death grip, oblivious to his blood-curdling screams for help. Then silence.

Slowly, the creature's hideous head sank back below the black waters of Lake Wicker.

"Lago da Morte!" Manolo whispered in terror. "Lago da Morte!"